GW00500818

NIHONGO NO KISO I

Foundations of Japanese
—English Translation—

THE ASSOCIATION FOR OVERSEAS TECHNICAL SCHOLARSHIP

This is the English translation of **NIHONGO NO KISO** I

All rights reserved
Copyright © by AOTS 1973

Edited by
Kaigai Gijutsusha Kenshū Kyōkai
(The Association for Overseas Technical Scholarship)
30-1, Senju-Azuma 1-chome, Adachi-ku, Tokyo 120, Japan

published by
3A Corporation
Shoei Bldg, 6-3, Sarugaku-cho 2 chome, Chiyoda-ku, Tokyo, 101 Japan
Printed in Japan

Preface

Since 1959, the Association for Overseas Technical Scholarship has hosted technical trainees from Asia, Africa and Latin America, totalling 17,526 as of March 1980.

Needless to say, the greatest obstacle that the overseas trainees have to overcome is the Japanese language. Without a good command of Japanese it is almost impossible to really enjoy life in Japan or to master technical problems. Experience shows us that the greater the trainee's language proficiency is, the more he learns from his technical training. The intensive Japanese course organized by this Association is an integral and important part of its 5-week Orientation Program given to the trainees before they start their technical training.

Our intensive Japanese course was originally a 3-week course. In 1961 it was extended to 5 weeks. There is a total of 100 instruction hours. This is obviously too short a period of time for acquisition of a language, but we are limited by the time allowed for the whole training program. Thus we have been facing the very serious problem of getting the most out of a short period of time.

Considering the situation of our trainees, we attempted to compile a suitable Japanese textbook of our own for them. It was published in 1961. And revised first in 1964, and again in 1965. Due to an increasing number of the trainees and their variety of educational backgrounds and nationalities, it proved necessary to revise completely this textbook. The result was *Practical Japanese Conversation* completed in 1967. Two years later, translations of the book in Spanish, Thai, Chinese, Korean and Indonesian were published. *Practical Japanese Conversation,* however, was gradually felt to contain too much grammar and vocabulary (app. 1300 words). We decided it was a little too involved to be used in our intensive course. After two years of careful examination and evaluation of our previous textbooks, we have compiled the present textbook **NIHONGO NO KISO**

With our ten years of experience in instruction and our constant research in both theory and practice, we now believe that this is the most appropriate textbook conceivable at the present time. If the student understands the organization and the aim of this textbook, and if he is faithful in his study, he can be assured of acquiring a high degree of proficiency in Japanese.

We would appreciate any recommendations or suggestions concerning the further improvement of this textbook.

About the Book

The Aim

1.   This textbook has been written by the Association for Overseas Technical Scholarship for its 5-week intensive course in Japanese of overseas trainees.

    The aim of this textbook is to help the beginner to acquire a speaking skill minimally essential for daily life in Japan. The Basic Sentence Patterns and vocabulary have been selected and arranged according to this purpose. The text is Romanized throughout to eliminate the burden of learning the Japanese writing system.

2.   It is assumed that the learner will use this textbook under a Japanese instructor's guidance. More emphasis is put on practical usage than on theoretical analyses. The sentence patterns and vocabulary have been selected according to the frequency of their usage, although special consideration has been given to the relative easiness with which the learner might understand and use them in the beginning stages.

3.   One of the characteristics of this textbook is that it presents what we might call the 'basic patterns for production skill'. They are estracted from a wide variety of sentence patterns used by the Japanese in daily conversations, and appropriately simplified and modified. Mastery of these patterns after intensive aural-oral practice, assures the learner of acquiring a sound speaking ability within a short period of time.

The Organization

1.   **NIHONGO NO KISO** comprises the Main Textbook, The Glossary and Translation, and a Grammatical Notes.

    The Main Textbook presents a brief explanation of Japanese pronunciation, thirty lessons, some songs, an Index and Charts.

2.   There are two editions of the Main Textbook: the one written in Roman characters, and the other written in the normal Japanese writing system, i.e. Chinese characters and Hiragana. No translation is given in the Main Textbook.

    It is desirable that the instructor conducts classes using as little of any other language as possible.

    There are ten versions of the Glossary and Translation, i.e. English, Indonesian, Thai, Spanish, Portuguese, Persian, Korean, Arabic, Chinese, and Vietnamese versions.

3. The patterns and words are arranged and carefully ordered in such a way that the learner can efficiently master all of them. The textbook contains a total of 763 words, the majority of which are from the lessons, although some words have added to provide a thorough understanding of the sentence patterns.

There will be a larger number of words introduced in the beginning, but the number will gradually decrease as the complexity of the patterns increases.

4. It will take at least three hours of class work to finish one lesson. If you finish one lesson a day, it will take at least five weeks (100 hours) of class work to complete all of the lessons as well as the Pronunciation Section.

Suggestions for the use

Following are brief accounts of content and aim of each section of the textbooks and some general suggestions for better use.

1. **About the Main Textbook:**

1) Pronunciation of Japanese

The first section for pronunciation is intended to be an aid for the beginners to familiarize themselves with the speech sounds of Japanese. It is advised to spend one or two hours on pronunciation practice before starting the lessons on sentence patterns.

2) The Lessons

A. Lesson 1 ～ 27

This part is the main body of the textbook. Each lesson is organized in the following way:

a) Sentence pattern

Presented at the beginning of each lesson are a few simple sentences which show the basic 'patterns' of expressions to be learnt in the lesson. You can create a variety of sentences by substituting the words in the pattern.

b) Conversation

This section presents conversational expressions which utilize the basic patterns according to various situations in daily life. It also introduces some idiomatic expressions useful to carry on daily conversation. It is important to practice the expressions and memorize them with close association with actual situations.

c) Example sentences

Here you find the basic patterns arranged in question-and-answer forms. Repeat the practice until you are able to answer the questions promptly. You should also become able to produce the questions corresponding to the statements.

d) Drill

The drill should always be aural-oral. Keep the textbook closed in the class, and follow what the instructor says. Practice should be repeated until you can use the basic patterns automatically. It would be advisable to use a tape recorder to improve yourself outside the classroom.

There are basically three different types of drill; substitution, transformation, and question-and-answer drills. Part A of the drill section consists of comparatively simple substitution and transformation drills, and Part B includes more complicated ones of essentially the same type, question-and-answer drills and mixture of different types of drills.

e) Questions

At the end of each lesson, there are some questions, ones concerning the grammar, and the others concerning the content of the lesson. (fill the blanks with appropriate words, etc.)

The purpose of this section if of course to secure the thorough understanding of the basic grammatical rules working in the expression presented in each lesson, and to make sure that you express yourself utilizing the patterns and vocabulary orally as well as in the written form.

f) Reviews

Lesson 24 and 26 have review practice on particles and conjugation patterns.

B. Lesson 28 ~ 30

Lesson 28 gives a summary of all the important particles, Lesson 29, a summary of conjugation patterns of verbs and adjectives, and Lesson 30, a summary of shifting of parts of speech, e.g. changing an adjective into a noun, etc.

All the important particles are introduced in the first thirteen lessons, so that it is advised to study Lesson 28 after finishing Lesson 13.

All the conjugated forms of verbs and adjectives appear in Lesson 13 through Lesson 19. Study Lesson 29 after finishing Lesson 19 for an overall review of conjugation.

Shifting of parts of speech, in other words, interrelations between nouns, adjectives, or verbs created out of the common base, appear Lesson 30 will give you an idea of how some adjectives, nouns or verbs are formally interrelated. It may be studied at any stage between Lesson 20 and Lesson 27.

3) Charts

The charts attached at the end of the book are supposed to be used to help build up a visual association between the expressions and the situations in oral drills. Make use of the charts always and try not to 'read' the sentences in the book.

2. **About the Separate Volume:**

The Separate Volume contains:

1) vocabulary (with translation)
2) translations of the basic pattern sentences, conversations and example sentences of the lessons
3) lists of numerals, auxiliary numerals, expressions of time and names of members of the family
4) lists of conjugated forms of verbs

You should always bear in mind that, strictly speaking, there is no one-to-one equivalents between Japanese and your language. Translations given in this book are merely to give you a rough idea of what the words or sentences mean. Although the instructor may sometimes use expressions in English or in your language to have you produce Japanese expressions, try as much as possible not to think that a particular Japanese word corresponds, one to one, to a particular word in English or in your language.

3. **About the Grammatical Notes:**

A brief explanation on the grammatical principles of each lesson is given in English.

4. **Supplement**

Some questions naturally expect different answers from different persons; the model answers are shown here assuming that a person named Slamet from Indonesia is answering.

5. **Notes on spelling and notation:**

1) The transcription ('spelling') adopted in the textbook is what is commonly called the 'Hepburn System (of Romanization)' with some minor modifications.

The bar over a vowel (e.g. ā, ū), shows a 'long' vowel. The long i, however, is spelled 'ii', instead of 'ī'. The distinction between the long and short (ordinary) vowels is very important in Japanese, so always pay attention to the presence and absence of the bar for all the vowels.

2) Capital letters are used at the beginning of a sentence and for proper names, just like in English.

e.g. Lee-san, Chūgoku, Nagoya, Indoneshia-go

3) Prefixes and suffixes are connected with the base with hyphens.

  e.g. o-shigoto, Tanaka-san, 25-sai

4) Words of foreign origin, including the names of countries are spelled according to the Japanese pronunciation.

  e.g. tape recorder → tēpu-rekōdā Mexico → Mekishiko

However, personal names are spelled in the same way as they are spelled (Romanized) in the country.

5) Omittable words are indicated with a [ ].

  e.g. Anata wa kenshūsei desu ka.

   − Hai, [watashi wa] kenshūsei desu.

6) Alternative words or expressions are shown in ( ).

  e.g. Anata wa dare (donata) desu ka.

6. Miscellaneous remarks:

This textbook uses only countries and the peoples of developing countries in Asia, Africa and Latin America. This is because our textbook has been written for the technical trainees from these countries.

The word 'Sentā' which often appears in this textbook refers to a regional center of the Association for Overseas Technical Scholarship. The Association has at present the following centers:

Tokyo Kenshu Center (at Tokyo)

Yokohama Kenshu Center (at Yokohama)

Kansai Kenshu Center (at Osaka)

Chubu Kenshu Center (at Nagoya)

Other General Advices to the Students

1. Practice basic patterns of expression repeatedly.

Needless to say, you cannot learn any language effectively without knowing the general rules — a grammar. It is also true, however, that the best way to become a good speaker of the language is to accept the expressions as they are, memorize them, and use them as often as possible, rather than worry about grammar all the time. This textbook is organized and arranged in such a way that the student will naturally acquire exact knowledge of how the language actually works by practicing the patterns repeatedly.

2. Listen to the correct pronunciation.

The Romanized letters do not necessarily express the correct sounds. Always listen to the correct pronunciation of the instructor or the tape and try to remember it.

3. Make good use of the class.

Language study is, of course, not limited only to the classroom but the best way is to learn with the instructor and the fellow students in a classroom. This textbook is composed to enable you to study the basis of Japanese language efficiently and systematically in 100 hours. Each lesson is a new lesson and quite important, so listen to the instructor attentively and practice with loud voice according to his instructions in the class.

4. Don't forget to review.

It is impossible to understand and remember only by going to class. Even if you can memorize many things at a time, you will forget them soon. So, after the class, review as long as possible by listening to the tapes and pronouncing by yourself. Generally speaking, after 3 hours of classroom study, it is necessary to review for 3 hours.

5. Try to use the words and the patterns as much as possible.

The base of language study is to remember and to use what you remember. Memorize the words and conversation of each lesson, and speak to your friends and to Japanese people using words and sentences which you have remembered. If you are ashamed to speak to in Japanese, you cannot improve your conversation ability.

6. After finishing this textbook.

If you use this text following the advices above, you should be able to master basic expressions and basic words necessary for daily life. You should be able to express most of what you want to say.

At first, you may have trouble comprehending what people say as you will be encountering many words which you don't know. But continue to speak and listen and patiently memorize words, and you will eventually understand the Japanese language as it is used by the Japanese people.

CONTENTS

Terms used for instruction

bunpō	ぶんぽう	grammar
hatsuon	はつおん	pronunciation
bun	ぶん	sentence
tango	たんご	word
onsetsu	おんせつ	syllable
boin	ぼいん	vowel
shi'in	しいん	consonant
nijū shi'in	にじゅうしいん	double consonant
dai〜ka	だい〜か	lesson 〜
bunkei	ぶんけい	sentence pattern
kaiwa	かいわ	conversation
reibun	れいぶん	example sentence
renshū	れんしゅう	practice
mondai	もんだい	exercise
fukushū	ふくしゅう	review
shitsumon	しつもん	question
kotae	こたえ	answer
rei	れい	example
reigai	れいがい	exception
hantai	はんたい	opposition
hon'yaku	ほんやく	translation
meishi	めいし	noun
dōshi	どうし	verb
i-keiyōshi	いけいようし	i-adjective
na-keiyōshi	なけいようし	na-adjective
joshi	じょし	particle
fukushi	ふくし	adverb
sūji	すうじ	numerals
josūshi	じょすうし	auxiliary numerals
gimonshi	ぎもんし	interrogative
kōzoku-ku	こうぞくく	a set of particular forms (words or phrases) always used after some conjugated forms of verbs or adjectives
genzai	げんざい	present or non-perfect
kako	かこ	past or perfect
kōtei	こうてい	affirmative
hitei	ひてい	negative
katei	かてい	conditional
ikō	いこう	volitional
-gurūpu	-グループ	-group
-kei	-けい	-form
teinei-tai	ていねいたい	polite style of speech
futsū-tai	ふつうたい	plain style of speech
chāto	チャート	chart
sakuin	さくいん	index

PART I

Vocabulary

Lesson 1

watashi	わたし	I
watashi-tachi	わたしたち	we
anata	あなた	you
anata-gata	あなたがた	you (plural)
sensei	せんせい	teacher
kenshūsei	けんしゅうせい	trainee
-san	－さん	Mr. Mrs. Miss
dare (donata)	だれ（どなた）	who
hai	はい	yes
iie	いいえ	no
sō	そう	so
Burajiru	ブラジル	Brazil
Chūgoku	ちゅうごく	China
Echiopia	エチオピア	Ethiopia
Firipin	フィリピン	Philippines
Indo	インド	India
Indoneshia	インドネシア	Indonesia
Iran	イラン	Iran
Kankoku	かんこく	Korea
Mekishiko	メキシコ	Mexico
Nihon	にほん	Japan
Ōsutoraria	オーストラリア	Australia
Perū	ペルー	Peru
Tai	タイ	Thailand
-jin	－じん	-people

kikai	きかい	machine

Ohayō gozaimasu.   Good morning.
   おはよう ございます。

Dōzo yoroshiku.   How do you do?
   どうぞ よろしく。

Lesson 2

kore	これ	this thing here
sore	それ	that thing near you
are	あれ	that thing over there
kono	この	this ~
sono	その	that ~
ano	あの	that ~
kono hito	このひと	this person
sono hito	そのひと	that person
ano hito	あのひと	that person
hon	ほん	book
zasshi	ざっし	magazine
jisho	じしょ	dictionary
nōto	ノート	notebook
kami	かみ	paper
shinbun	しんぶん	newspaper
pen	ペン	pen
bōrupen	ボールペン	ball-point pen
enpitsu	えんぴつ	pencil
tabako	タバコ	tabacco
matchi	マッチ	matches
haizara	はいざら	ash tray
kagi	かぎ	key
tokei	とけい	watch, clock
hako	はこ	box
kaban	かばん	bag

isu	いす	chair
tsukue	つくえ	desk
mado	まど	window
doa	ドア	door
rajio	ラジオ	radio
terebi	テレビ	television
kamera	カメラ	camera
denki	でんき	electricity
jidōsha	じどうしゃ	automobile
namae	なまえ	name
senmon	せんもん	speciality
nan	なん	what
-sai	ーさい	-years old
o-ikutsu (nan-sai)	おいくつ（なんさい）	how old
-ban	ーばん	No.
hyaku	ひゃく	hundred

*　　*　　*　　*　　*

[Kagi o] kudasai.　　　　　　Please give me [the key].
　[かぎを] ください。

Chotto matte kudasai.　　　　Please wait a moment.
　ちょっと まって ください。

Hai, dōzo.　　　　　　　　　Yes, please.
　はい、どうぞ。

[Dōmo] arigatō gozaimasu.　　Thank you [very much].
　[どうも] ありがとう ございます。

Dō itashimashite.　　　　　　You're welcome.　Not at all.
　どう いたしまして。

— 5 —

Lesson 3

koko	ここ	here, this place
soko	そこ	there, that place near you
asoko	あそこ	that place over there
doko	どこ	where
kochira	こちら	this way (direction)
sochira	そちら	that way (direction)
achira	あちら	that way (direction)
dochira	どちら	which way (direction)
kyōshitsu	きょうしつ	classroom
shokudō	しょくどう	dining hall
otearai	おてあらい	toilet
robii	ロビー	lobby
uketsuke	うけつけ	information desk
jimusho	じむしょ	office
heya	へや	room
niwa	にわ	garden
[Kenshū] Sentā	[けんしゅう]センター	the center [for the trainees]
uchi	うち	house
kaisha	かいしゃ	company
kuni	くに	country
Suisu	スイス	Switzerland
Amerika	アメリカ	the United States of America
Igirisu	イギリス	England
denwa	でんわ	telephone
kagaku	かがく	chemistry

Arabia-go	アラビアご	Arabic
Chūgoku-go	ちゅうごくご	Chinese
Ei-go	えいご	English
Nihon-go	にほんご	Japanese
Supein-go	スペインご	Spanish
-go	−ご	-language
～to～	～と～	and (connects nouns)
soshite	そして	and (connects sentences)
-en	−えん	-yen
ikura	いくら	how much
sen	せん	1,000
ichi-man	いちまん	10,000
jū-man	じゅうまん	100,000
hyaku-man	ひゃくまん	1,000,000

*　　*　　*　　*　　*

dewa	では	then

Kon'nichiwa.
こんにちは。

Good afternoon.

Chigaimasu.
ちがいます。

It is not so.　It is wrong.

Sō desu ka.
そうですか。

It that so ?　I see.

[Lee-san to] onaji desu ne.
［リーさんと］おなじですね。

It is the same [as Mr. Lee's,] isn't it ?

Lesson 4

okimasu	おきます	get up
nemasu	ねます	go to bed, sleep
hatarakimasu	はたらきます	work
yasumimasu	やすみます	take a rest
benkyō-shimasu	べんきょうします	study
ima	いま	now
chōdo	ちょうど	just
-ji	−じ	-o'clock
-fun (-pun)	−ふん（−ぷん）	-minutes
han	はん	half (30 minutes)
nan-ji	なんじ	what time
nan-pun	なんぷん	how many minutes
gozen	ごぜん	a.m.
gogo	ごご	p.m.
asa	あさ	morning
hiru	ひる	daytime, noon
ban (yoru)	ばん（よる）	night, evening
ototoi	おととい	the day before yesterday
kinō	きのう	yesterday
kyō	きょう	today
ashita	あした	tomorrow
asatte	あさって	the day after tomorrow
kesa	けさ	this morning
konban	こんばん	tonight

~kara	～から	from ～
~made	～まで	to ～
nichi-yōbi	にちようび	Sunday
getsu-yōbi	げつようび	Monday
ka-yōbi	かようび	Tuesday
sui-yōbi	すいようび	Wednesday
moku-yōbi	もくようび	Thursday
kin-yōbi	きんようび	Friday
do-yōbi	どようび	Saturday
nan-yōbi	なんようび	what day of the week
~[no] tsugi	～[の] つぎ	next [to] ～

* * * * *

ocha	おちゃ	tea
benkyō	べんきょう	study (noun)

Konbanwa.
こんばんは。

Good Evening.

Dōzo, kochira e.
どうぞ、こちらへ。

This way, please.

[Ocha wa] ikaga desu ka.
[おちゃは] いかがですか。

How would you like [tea]?
How about [tea]?

[Sore wa] taihen desu ne.
[それは] たいへんですね。

That's awful, isn't it?

Lesson 5

ikimasu	いきます	go
kimasu	きます	come
kaerimasu	かえります	go home, return
kōjō	こうじょう	factory
eki	えき	station
ginkō	ぎんこう	bank
byōin	びょういん	hospital
depāto	デパート	department store
hon-ya	ほんや	book store
toko-ya	とこや	barber
-ya	ーや	—store
1-gatsu	いちがつ	January
2-gatsu	にがつ	February
3-gatsu	さんがつ	March
4(shi)-gatsu	しがつ	April
5-gatsu	ごがつ	May
6-gatsu	ろくがつ	June
7(shichi)-gatsu	しちがつ	July
8-gatsu	はちがつ	August
9(ku)-gatsu	くがつ	September
10-gatsu	じゅうがつ	October
11-gatsu	じゅういちがつ	November
12-gatsu	じゅうにがつ	December
-nichi	ーにち	—th day
tanjōbi	たんじょうび	birthday

nan-gatsu	なんがつ	which month
nan-nichi	なんにち	what day of the month
itsu	いつ	when
hikōki	ひこうき	airplane
fune	ふね	ship
densha	でんしゃ	electric train
basu	バス	bus
takushii	タクシー	taxi
chikatetsu	ちかてつ	subway
shinkansen	しんかんせん	New Main Line, super express train
aruite	あるいて	on foot
hito	ひと	person
tomodachi	ともだち	friend
koibito	こいびと	sweetheart
issho ni	いっしょに	together
hitori de	ひとりで	alone
senshū	せんしゅう	last week
konshū	こんしゅう	this week
raishū	らいしゅう	next week
sengetsu	せんげつ	last month
kongetsu	こんげつ	this month
raigetsu	らいげつ	next month
kyonen	きょねん	last year
kotoshi	ことし	this year
rainen	らいねん	next year

* * * * *

[O-]genki desu ka.
 [お]げんきですか。 — How are you?　Are you well?

[Anata wa] dō desu ka.
 [あなたは]どうですか。 — How are you?

[Sore wa] ii desu ne.
 [それは]いいですね。 — That's nice, isn't it?

Lesson 6

tabemasu	たべます	eat
kaimasu	かいます	buy
suimasu [tabako o —]	すいます [タバコを —]	smoke
nomimasu	のみます	drink
torimasu [shashin o —]	とります [しゃしんを —]	take [a photo]
kikimasu	ききます	listen
yomimasu	よみます	read
kakimasu	かきます	write
mimasu	みます	see
jisshū-shimasu	じっしゅうします	have a practical training
pinpon-shimasu	ピンポンします	play pingpong
shimasu	します	do
hajimemasu	はじめます	begin
owarimasu	おわります	finish, come to an end
gohan	ごはん	meal, rice
asagohan	あさごはん	breakfast
hirugohan	ひるごはん	lunch
bangohan	ばんごはん	supper
pan	パン	bread
tamago	たまご	egg
niku	にく	meat
sakana	さかな	fish
yasai	やさい	vegetable
kudamono	くだもの	fruits
ringo	りんご	apple
gyūnyū (miruku)	ぎゅうにゅう （ミルク）	milk

kōhii	コーヒー	coffee
kōcha	こうちゃ	black tea
jūsu	ジュース	juice
mizu	みず	water
biiru	ビール	beer
[o-]sake	[お]さけ	liquor, *sake*
kippu	きっぷ	ticket
nekutai	ネクタイ	necktie
shatsu	シャツ	shirt
kutsu	くつ	shoes
hana	はな	flower
kusuri	くすり	medicine
kitte	きって	postage stamp
fūtō	ふうとう	envelope
nani	なに	what
tegami	てがみ	letter
eiga	えいが	movie
shashin	しゃしん	photo
kōgi	こうぎ	lecture
rekōdo	レコード	record
maiasa	まいあさ	every morning
maiban	まいばん	every night
mainichi	まいにち	every day

* * * * *

-jikan	-じかん	–hours
donokurai	どのくらい	about how much (many)
kakarimasu	かかります	take (time)

Lesson 7

kirimasu	きります	cut
shūri-shimasu	しゅうりします	repair
agemasu	あげます	give
kashimasu	かします	lend
okurimasu	おくります	send
oshiemasu	おしえます	teach
kakemasu	かけます	make a phone call
[denwa o —]	[でんわを —]	
moraimasu	もらいます	receive
naraimasu	ならいます	learn
hashi	はし	chopsticks
naifu	ナイフ	knife
fōku	フォーク	fork
supūn	スプーン	spoon
te	て	hand
doraibā	ドライバー	screw driver
supana	スパナ	spanners
penchi	ペンチ	cutting pliers
okane	おかね	money
repōto	レポート	report
katarogu	カタログ	catalogue
nimotsu	にもつ	baggage
otōsan	おとうさん	father
okāsan	おかあさん	mother
oniisan	おにいさん	elder brother
onēsan	おねえさん	elder sister
otōto	おとうと	younger brother
imōto	いもうと	younger sister

okusan	おくさん	wife
kodomo	こども	child
mō	もう	already
mada [. . . masen]	まだ［…ません］	(not) yet
Oyasuminasai.	おやすみなさい。	Good night.
Sayōnara.	さようなら。	Good-bye.

*   *   *   *   *

ea-mēru	エアメール	air mail
-kiro	ーキロ	–kilo (grams, meters)
ē	ええ	yes
tsukimasu	つきます	arrive

[Chotto] sumimasen.　　　　　　Excuse me.　I am sorry.
　［ちょっと］すみません。

Daijōbu desu.　　　　　　　　　That's nothing to worry about.
　だいじょうぶです。

Onegai-shimasu.　　　　　　　　I ask your favor.
　おねがいします。

Lesson 8

kirei(-na)	きれい（な）	beautiful, clean
hansamu(-na)	ハンサム（な）	handsome
shinsetsu(-na)	しんせつ（な）	kind
genki(-na)	げんき（な）	healthy, cheerful
yūmei(-na)	ゆうめい（な）	famous
shizuka(-na)	しずか（な）	quiet
ōkii	おおきい	big, large
chiisai	ちいさい	small, little
atarashii	あたらしい	new
furui	ふるい	old (not of age)
ii (yoi)	いい（よい）	good
warui	わるい	bad
atsui	あつい	hot
samui	さむい	cold (weather)
tsumetai	つめたい	cold (things)
muzukashii	むずかしい	difficult
yasashii	やさしい	easy
takai	たかい	high, expensive
hikui	ひくい	low
yasui	やすい	cheap
omoshiroi	おもしろい	interesting
oishii	おいしい	tasty, delicious
shiroi	しろい	white
kuroi	くろい	black
akai	あかい	red
aoi	あおい	blue
sakura	さくら	cherry blossom

shiken	しけん	examination
tabemono	たべもの	food
machi	まち	town, city
tokoro	ところ	place
yama	やま	mountain
donna	どんな	what kind of
dō	どう	how
taihen	たいへん	very
amari [...masen]	あまり [...ません]	(not) so

*   *   *   *   *

～ga,	～が、	but

aimasu [tomodachi ni —]   meet [a friend]
　あいます [ともだちに —]

Tadaima.   I'm home now.
　ただいま。

Okaerinasai.   Nice to see you back.
　おかえりなさい。

Lesson 9

wakarimasu	わかります	understand
arimasu	あります	have
suki(-na)	すき（な）	like
kirai(-na)	きらい（な）	dislike
jōzu(-na)	じょうず（な）	be good at
heta(-na)	へた（な）	be poor at
hiragana	ひらがな	the 'Hiragana' transcription
katakana	かたかな	the 'Katakana' transcription
rōmaji	ローマじ	the Roman alphabet
kanji	かんじ	Chinese character
imi	いみ	meaning
taipu	タイプ	typewriter, typewriting
tsukai-kata	つかいかた	how to use
butaniku	ぶたにく	pork, pig-meat
toriniku	とりにく	chicken, chicken-meat
gyūniku	ぎゅうにく	beef, cow-meat
nomimono	のみもの	drinks
ryōri	りょうり	dish, cooking
dansu	ダンス	dancing
uta	うた	song
ongaku	おんがく	music
supōtsu	スポーツ	sports
tenisu	テニス	tennis
gitā	ギター	guitar

yoku	よく		well
zenzen [...masen]	ぜんぜん [...ません]		(not) at all
takusan	たくさん		much, many
sukoshi	すこし		a little, a few
~dake	~だけ		only
mochiron	もちろん		of course
dōshite	どうして		why, how
~kara,	~から、		because ~
netsu	ねつ		fever
atama	あたま		head
onaka	おなか		stomach
byōki	びょうき		illness
itai	いたい		have ~ache
yasumimasu	やすみます		take a day off
[kaisha o —]	[かいしゃを —]		[from company]

* * * * *

chūsha	ちゅうしゃ		injection

Dō shimashita ka.   What's the matter (with you)?
　どう しましたか。

[Watashi wa] kaze o hikimashita. I've caught cold.
　[わたしは] かぜを ひきました。

[Watashi wa] atama ga itai desu. I have a headache.
　[わたしは] あたまが いたいです。

Lesson 10

imasu	います	there is (animate being)
arimasu	あります	there is (inanimate thing)
ue	うえ	on, above, up
shita	した	under, below, beneath
naka	なか	in, inside
soto	そと	outside
mae	まえ	front
ushiro	うしろ	behind, back
migi	みぎ	right
hidari	ひだり	left
tonari	となり	next (door)
chikaku	ちかく	near
aida	あいだ	between, among
boruto	ボルト	bolt
natto	ナット	nut
suitchi	スイッチ	switch
pasupōto	パスポート	passport
otoko no hito	おとこの ひと	man
onna no hito	おんなの ひと	woman
kōen	こうえん	park
gakkō	がっこう	school
resutoran	レストラン	restaurant
biru	ビル	building
posuto	ポスト	post box
yūbinkyoku	ゆうびんきょく	post office
taishikan	たいしかん	embassy

iroiro　　　　　いろいろ　　　　　　　　　　various

~ya~ [...nado]　~や~ [...など]　　　and so on

-kai　　　　　　－かい　　　　　　　　　　-th floor

　　　　　　　*　　*　　*　　*　　*

korekara　　　これから　　　　　　　　from now on

Itte irasshai.　　　　　　　　　Hurry back. (a greeting used
　いって いらっしゃい。　　　　　　when seeing someone off)

Itte mairimasu.　　　　　　　　I'm going. (a greeting used by
　いって まいります。　　　　　　　a person who is leaving)

Lesson 11

imasu	います	stay
sentaku-shimasu	せんたくします	wash (clothes)
sōji-shimasu	そうじします	clean (room)
hitotsu	ひとつ	one (thing)
futatsu	ふたつ	two
mittsu	みっつ	three
yottsu	よっつ	four
itsutsu	いつつ	five
muttsu	むっつ	six
nanatsu	ななつ	seven
yattsu	やっつ	eight
kokonotsu	ここのつ	nine
tō	とお	ten
ikutsu	いくつ	how many
hitori	ひとり	one person
futari	ふたり	two persons
3-nin	さんにん	three persons
-nin	-にん	-persons
kazoku	かぞく	family
kyōdai	きょうだい	brothers & sisters
-shūkan	-しゅうかん	-weeks
-kagetsu	-かげつ	-months
-nen	-ねん	-years
-kai	-かい	-times

zenbu de	ぜんぶで	in all
daitai	だいたい	about, roughly
〜gurai (kurai)	〜ぐらい（くらい）	about 〜
-dai	−だい	auxiliary numeral for machine etc.
-mai	−まい	auxiliary numeral for paper

*   *   *   *   *

gaikoku	がいこく	foreign country
[Nihon]-sei	［にほん］せい	made in [Japan]
zenbu	ぜんぶ	all
tsukurimasu	つくります	produce, make

Lesson 12

chikai	ちかい	near
tōi	とおい	far
hayai	はやい	fast
osoi	おそい	slow
ōi [hito ga —]	おおい [ひとが —]	many [people]
sukunai [hito ga —]	すくない [ひとが —]	few [people]
atatakai	あたたかい	warm
suzushii	すずしい	cool
omoi	おもい	heavy
karui	かるい	light
nagai	ながい	long
mijikai	みじかい	short
amai	あまい	sweet
karai	からい	salty, hot (taste)
isogashii	いそがしい	busy
hima(-na)	ひま(な)	free (time)
wakai	わかい	young
toshi-ue	としうえ	elder
tanoshii	たのしい	enjoyable, pleasant, happy
taisetsu(-na)	たいせつ(な)	important, precious
dochira	どちら	which (two)
dore	どれ	which (three & over)
ichiban	いちばん	the most, Number one
onaji	おなじ	same
ryōhō	りょうほう	both
kawa	かわ	river

sekai	せかい	world
kurasu	クラス	class
mikan	みかん	orange
ame	あめ	rain
kumori	くもり	cloudy
[o-]tenki	[お]てんき	weather
ryokō	りょこう	trip, tour
yasumi	やすみ	holiday

* * * * *

[o-]shigoto	[お]しごと	work, business
itsumo	いつも	always, usually
tokidoki	ときどき	sometimes
~goro	~ごろ	about (time)

Ii o-tenki desu ne.　　　Very nice weather, isn't it?
　いい おてんきですね。

Sō desu ne.　　　Let me see.
　そうですね。

Lesson 13

asobimasu I (asobu, asonde)   enjoy oneself, play
　あそびます（あそぶ，あそんで）
kaemasu II (kaeru, kaete)   change (v.t.)
　かえます（かえる，かえて）
dashimasu [tegami o —] I (dasu, dashite) send [a letter]
　だします［てがみ を —］（だす，だして）
kekkon-shimasu III (-suru, -shite)   marry
　けっこんします（−する，−して）
kenbutsu-shimasu III (-suru, -shite)   do sightseeing
　けんぶつします　（−する，−して）
kengaku-shimasu III (-suru, -shite)   visit (factories, schools,
　けんがくします　（−する，−して）   etc.)
kaimono-shimasu III (-suru, -shite)   do shopping
　かいものします　（−する，−して）
sanpo-shimasu III (-suru, -shite)   take a walk
　さんぽします　（−する，−して）

hoshii   ほしい   want (to have)

toranjisutā-rajio   トランジスターラジオ   transister radio
tēpu-rekōdā   テープレコーダー   tape recorder
kasetto   カセット   cassette
karā-terebi   カラーテレビ   color television
[o-]miyage   ［お］みやげ   souvenir

erebētā   エレベーター   elevator
kōjō-kengaku   こうじょうけんがく   visiting a factory

demo   でも   but

　　　　　　*　　　*　　　*　　　*　　　*

hairimasu [heya ni —] I (hairu, haitte)   enter [the room]
　はいります［へやに —］（はいる，はいって）

demasu [heya o —] II (deru, dete)　　　　go out [of the room]
でます ［へやを ―］ 　（でる，でて）

Tsukaremashita.　　　　　　　　　　　　　[I am] tired.
　つかれました。
[Watashi wa] nodo ga kawakimashita.　　　[I am] thirsty.
　［わたしは］のどが かわきました。
[Watashi wa] onaka ga sukimashita.　　　　[I am] hungry.
　［わたしは］おなかが すきました。
[Watashi wa] onaka ga ippai desu.　　　　　[I am] full.
　［わたしは］おなかが いっぱい です。

Lesson 14

hanashimasu I (hanasu, hanashite)   speak, talk
はなします（はなす，はなして）

machimasu I (matsu, matte)   wait
まちます（まつ，まって）

tachimasu I (tatsu, tatte)   stand up
たちます（たつ，たって）

torimasu I (toru, totte)   take
とります（とる，とって）

iimasu I (iu, itte)   say
いいます（いう，いって）

isogimasu I (isogu, isoide)   hurry
いそぎます（いそぐ，いそいで）

yobimasu I (yobu, yonde)   call
よびます（よぶ，よんで）

misemasu II (miseru, misete)   show
みせます（みせる，みせて）

oboemasu II (oboeru, oboete)   memorize, remember
おぼえます（おぼえる，おぼえて）

oshiemasu II (oshieru, oshiete)   tell
おしえます（おしえる，おしえて）

furimasu [ame ga —] I (furu, futte)   it rains
ふります［あめが —］（ふる，ふって）

jikan	じかん	time
jūsho	じゅうしょ	address
denwa-bangō	でんわばんごう	telephone number
shio	しお	salt
satō	さとう	sugar
hakkiri	はっきり	clearly
yukkuri	ゆっくり	slowly

mō ichido	もう いちど	once again
motto	もっと	more
hayaku	はやく	fast (adv.)
chotto	ちょっと	a little

* * * * *

mise	みせ	shop, store

Irasshai[mase].　　Welcome. (a geeting to a customer
　いらっしゃい[ませ]。　　or a guest coming in)

Lesson 15

suwarimasu I (suwaru, suwatte) すわります（すわる，すわって）	sit down
tsukaimasu I (tsukau, tsukatte) つかいます（つかう，つかって）	use
tetsudaimasu I (tetsudau, tetsudatte) てつだいます（てつだう，てつだって）	help (one's work)
okimasu I (oku, oite) おきます（おく，おいて）	put
tsukemasu II (tsukeru, tsukete) つけます（つける，つけて）	switch on, attach
keshimasu I (kesu, keshite) けします（けす，けして）	switch off, erase
akemasu II (akeru, akete) あけます（あける，あけて）	open
shimemasu II (shimeru, shimete) しめます（しめる，しめて）	shut
mochimasu I (motsu, motte) もちます（もつ，もって）	hold
shirimasu I (shiru, shitte) しります（しる，しって）	get to know
sumimasu I (sumu, sunde) すみます（すむ，すんで）	live, inhabit
urimasu I (uru, utte) うります（うる，うって）	sell
kimasu II (kiru, kite) きます（きる，きて）	wear
narimasu I (naru, natte) なります（なる，なって）	become
motte imasu　もって います	have, possess
shitte imasu　しって います	know
sunde imasu　すんで います	live (in Tokyo, etc.), reside

kasa	かさ		umbrella
sekken	せっけん		soap
taoru	タオル		towel
fuku	ふく		dress, clothes
akarui	あかるい		bright
kurai	くらい		dark
dandan	だんだん		gradually
soredewa	それでは		well, then

*   *   *   *   *

dokushin	どくしん		single, not married

Lesson 16

kaeshimasu I (kaesu, kaeshite)		give back, return
かえします（かえす，かえして）		
arukimasu I (aruku, aruite)		walk
あるきます（あるく，あるいて）		
haraimasu I (harau, haratte)		pay
はらいます（はらう，はらって）		
norimasu [densha ni —] I (noru, notte)		get on, ride
のります［でんしゃに —］（のる，のって）		［an electric train］
orimasu [densha o —] II (oriru, orite)		get off [an electric train]
おります［でんしゃを —］（おりる，おりて）		
tomarimasu I (tomaru, tomatte)		stop (v.i.)
とまります（とまる，とまって）		

hiroi	ひろい	wide
semai	せまい	narrow
benri(-na)	べんり（な）	convenient, useful, handy
kantan(-na)	かんたん（な）	simple

se ga takai	せが たかい	tall (a person or an animal)
yaku ni tachimasu	やくに たちます	be useful

sorekara	それから	after that

kao	かお	face
me	め	eye
hana	はな	nose
kuchi	くち	mouth
mimi	みみ	ear
ha	は	tooth
kami	かみ	hair
ashi	あし	leg, foot

```
              *      *      *      *      *
purēyā        プレーヤー              record player
oto           おと                    sound
sugu          すぐ                    immediately
ato de        あと で                 later
jā            じゃあ                   then


irimasu ［purēyā ga —］ | (iru, itte)        need ［a record player］,
   いります ［プレーヤーが —］（いる，いって）    necessary
komarimasu | (komaru, komatte)              be troubled
   こまります（こまる，こまって）


［Sore wa］ komarimasu.          It's not OK for me.
   ［それは］こまります。
```

Lesson 17

nakushimasu I (nakusu, nakushite) なくします (なくす, なくして)		lose
sawarimasu I (sawaru, sawatte) さわります (さわる, さわって)		touch
waraimasu I (warau, waratte) わらいます (わらう, わらって)		laugh, smile
nugimasu I (nugu, nuide) ぬぎます (ぬぐ, ぬいで)		take off (clothes, shoes, etc.)
wasuremasu II (wasureru, wasurete) わすれます (わすれる, わすれて)		forget
iremasu II (ireru, irete) いれます (いれる, いれて)		put in
dashimasu I (dasu, dashite) だします (だす, だして)		put out, take out
tomemasu II (tomeru, tomete) とめます (とめる, とめて)		stop (v.t.)
shinpai-shimasu III (-suru, -shite) しんぱいします (-する, -して)		worry
ki o tsukemasu	きを つけます	pay attention
motte ikimasu	もって いきます	take something with someone
motte kimasu	もって きます	bring, fetch
kotoba	ことば	language, word
abunai	あぶない	dangerous
desukara (dakara)	ですから (だから)	therefore
hayaku	はやく	early
osoku	おそく	late (adv.)

＊　　　＊　　　＊　　　＊　　　＊

yā	やあ	hello, hi, oh
kega	けが	injury
karada	からだ	body, health

naorimasu I (naoru, naotte)　　　　　get well, recover
　なおります（なおる，なおって）

Gomen kudasai.　　　　　　May I come in ? (a greeting used
　ごめんください。　　　　　　by a visitor)
Shibaraku desu ne.　　　　　I haven't seen you for a long
　しばらくですね。　　　　　　time.
[Sore wa] yokatta desu ne.　It's nice. [wasn't it ?]
　[それは] よかったですね。
[Karada ni] ki o tsukete kudasai.　Take good care of yourself.
　[からだに] きを つけて ください。

Lesson 18

dekimasu II (dekiru, dekite)   can, be able
できます（できる，できて）

naoshimasu I (naosu, naoshite)   repair, mend
なおします（なおす，なおして）

hikimasu [gitā o —] I (hiku, hiite)   play [the guitar]
ひきます［ギターを —］（ひく，ひいて）

utaimasu [uta o —] I (utau, utatte)   sing [a song]
うたいます［うたを —］（うたう，うたって）

oyogimasu I (oyogu, oyoide)   swim
およぎます（およぐ，およいで）

unten-shimasu III (-suru, -shite)   drive
うんてんします（−する，−して）

karimasu II (kariru, karite)   borrow
かります（かりる，かりて）

araimasu I (arau, aratte)   wash
あらいます（あらう，あらって）

abimasu [shawā o —] II (abiru, abite) take shower
あびます［シャワーを —］（あびる，あびて）

dekakemasu II (dekakeru, dekakete)   go out
でかけます（でかける，でかけて）

nokku-shimasu III (-suru, -shite)   knock
ノックします（−する，−して）

koshō-shimasu III (-suru, -shite)   get out of order,
こしょうします（−する，−して）   break down

kuruma   くるま   vehicle
mētoru   メートル   meter

          *   *   *   *   *

[go-]shujin   ごしゅじん   (your/her) husband
Moshi moshi. もし もし。   Hello.(on the telephone)

[A-san wa] irasshaimasu ka.   Is Mr. A in ? (honorific)
  [A さんは] いらっしゃいますか。

[Sore wa] zannen desu.   I'm sorry to hear that.
  [それは] ざんねんです。

Yoroshiku itte kudasai.   Please give my best regards
  よろしく いって ください。   [to him].

[Dōzo] o-genki de.   Best of luck.
  [どうぞ] おげんきで。

Lesson 19

kikimasu [sensei ni —] I (kiku, kiite)   ask [the teacher]
   ききます [せんせいに —] (きく, きいて)
tomarimasu [hoteru ni —] I (tomaru, tomatte)   stay [at hotel]
   とまります [ホテルに —] (とまる, とまって)
yamemasu [tabako o —] II (yameru, yamete)   give up [smoking]
   やめます [タバコを —] (やめる, やめて)

kabuki	かぶき	a Japanese classical drama
sukiyaki	すきやき	Sukiyaki (a Japanese dish)
yuki	ゆき	snow
umi	うみ	sea
hoteru	ホテル	hotel
orientēshon	オリエンテーション	orientation
yoku	よく	often
-do	–ど	times
~ ka ~	~か~	or
tsugi no ~	つぎの ~	next, following
~[no] mae ni	~[の] まえに	before ~
~[no] ato de	~[の] あとで	after ~

*   *   *   *   *

ā	ああ	Ah! Oh!

Shitsurei desu ga,   Excuse me, but...
   しつれいですが、   I beg your pardon.
[Dōmo] shitsurei-shimashita. I'm sorry (that I've had no manners).
   [どうも] しつれいしました。
Iie, kamaimasen.   Never mind.
   いいえ、かまいません。

Hajimemashite, dōzo yoroshiku.　　I'm glad to meet you.
　はじめまして、どうぞ よろしく。

Kochira koso, dōzo yoroshiku.　　I'm glad to meet you.
　こちらこそ、どうぞ よろしく。　　So am I.

Lesson 20

nikki	にっき	diary

*   *   *   *   *

un	うん	yes (an informal equivalent of 'hai' used mainly by men)
kimi	きみ	you (an informal equivalent of 'anata' used by men)
boku	ぼく	I (an informal equivalent of 'watashi' used by men)

Lesson 21

omoimasu I (omou, omotte)　　　think, guess, suppose
　おもいます（おもう，おもって）

pātii	パーティー	party
minasan	みなさん	all of (you, them)
•kanai	かない	(my) wife

hijōni	ひじょうに	very, extremely
sonnani	そんなに	(not) so
[...masen]	[…ません]	
tabun	たぶん	probably
kitto	きっと	surely

Itadakimasu.	いただきます。	(a greeting before eating)
Gochisōsama.	ごちそうさま。	(a greeting after eating)

＊　　　＊　　　＊　　　＊　　　＊

[Nihon ni] tsuite		about [Japan],
	[にほんに] ついて	concerning [Japan]
mono	もの	thing
seihin	せいひん	product
tokuni	とくに	especially
zutto	ずっと	by far
shikashi	しかし	but
keredomo	けれども	but

Lesson 22

watarimasu I (wataru, watatte)		go across
わたります (わたる, わたって)		
magarimasu I (magaru, magatte)		turn (the corner)
まがります (まがる, まがって)		
chūi-shimasu [jidōsha ni —] III (-suru, -shite)		pay attention [to cars]
ちゅういします [じどうしゃに —] (する, して)		

kanashii	かなしい	sad
ureshii	うれしい	glad, happy
sabishii	さびしい	lonely
nemui	ねむい	sleepy

ōbā	オーバー	overcoat
sētā	セーター	sweater

Omedetō gozaimasu.	Congratulations.
おめでとう ございます。	

* * * * *

norikaemasu II (norikaeru, norikaete)		change (trains)
のりかえます (のりかえる, のりかえて)		

dōyatte	どうやって	how, in what way
massugu	まっすぐ	straight
michi	みち	way, road
kōsaten	こうさてん	crossing
hashi	はし	bridge

Lesson 23

umaremasu II (umareru, umarete) うまれます（うまれる，うまれて）		be born
shitsumon-shimasu III (-suru, -shite) しつもんします（－する，－して）		ask a question
futto bōru	フットボール	football
konoaida	このあいだ	the other day

*   *   *   *   *

kenshū-ryokō	けんしゅうりょこう	study tour
mēkā	メーカー	maker, manufacturer
kare	かれ	he
kanojo	かのじょ	she
ōkina	おおきな	big
chiisana	ちいさな	small
～[no] tsugi ni	～[の] つぎに	next to, after
hoka ni	ほかに	besides
sā	さあ	well, let me see

Lesson 24

kakimasu [e o —] I (kaku, kaite)   draw, paint [a picture]
  かきます [えを —] (かく, かいて)
kumitatemasu II (kumitateru, kumitatete)   assemble
  くみたてます (くみたてる, くみたてて)
bunkai-shimasu III (-suru, -shite)   take (a machine)
  ぶんかいします (ーする, ーして)   to pieces
setsumei-shimasu III (-suru, -shite)   explain
  せつめいします (ーする, ーして)

shumi   しゅみ   hobby
e   え   picture
yakyū   やきゅう   baseball

jibun de   じぶんで   by oneself
matawa   または   or, otherwise

        *   *   *   *   *

Hontō desu ka.   Is that true?
  ほんとうですか。
Ganbatte kudasai.   Try your best.
  がんばって ください。

Lesson 25

shirabemasu II (shiraberu, shirabete)   check up, investigate
　しらべます（しらべる，しらべて）

kangaemasu II (kangaeru, kangaete)   think
　かんがえます（かんがえる，かんがえて）

ichinichi-jū　　いちにちじゅう   all day long

moshi [...tara] もし［…たら］   if
ikura [...temo] いくら［…ても］   however

        *   *   *   *   *

ugokimasu I (ugoku, ugoite)   move, work
　うごきます（うごく，うごいて）

oshimasu I (osu, oshite)   push, press
　おします（おす，おして）

hikimasu I (hiku, hiite)   pull
　ひきます（ひく，ひいて）

tsukimasu I (tsuku, tsuite)   be turned on
　つきます（つく，ついて）

kiemasu II (kieru, kiete)   be turned off
　きえます（きえる，きえて）

botan　　ボタン   button
ranpu　　ランプ   lamp
tesutā　　テスター   tester

hajime ni　　はじめに   first, at the beginning
owari ni　　おわりに   last, at the end

soredemo　　それでも   still, and yet

Lesson 26

miemasu II (mieru, miete)		(can) be seen
みえます（みえる，みえて）		
kikoemasu II (kikoeru, kikoete)		(can) be heard
きこえます（きこえる，きこえて）		
dekimasu II (dekiru, dekite)		come into existence, be formed
できます（できる，できて）		
chōsetsu-shimasu III (-suru, -shite)		adjust
ちょうせつします（－する，－して）		
sōsa-shimasu III (-suru, -shite)		operate
そうさします（－する，－して）		
koe	こえ	voice
yūbe	ゆうべ	last night
itsuka	いつか	some day
mata	また	again
shika	しか	only, no more than
[...masen]	[...ません]	

* * * * *

shokuji-shimasu III (-suru, -shite)		have a meal, dine
しょくじします（－する，－して）		
made ni	までに	by, before

Lesson 27

kudasaimasu I (kudasaru, kudasatte)　　　[someone (respected)]
　くださいます（くださる，くださって）　　gives me (honorific)
irasshaimasu I (irassharu, irasshatte)　　　be, go, come (honorific)
いらっしゃいます（いらっしゃる，いらっしゃって）
osshaimasu I (ossharu, osshatte)　　　　say (honorific)
　おっしゃいます（おっしゃる，おっしゃって）
meshiagarimasu I (meshiagaru, meshiagatte)　eat, drink (honorific)
めしあがります（めしあがる，めしあがって）

kāten　　　　　カーテン　　　　　　　curtain

Oide kudasai.　おいで ください。　　Please come. (honorific)
O-kake kudasai.　おかけ ください。　　Please sit down. (honorific)

　　　　　＊　　＊　　＊　　＊　　＊

o-yasumi ni narimasu　　　　　　　take a rest, sleep
　おやすみに なります　　　　　　　　(honorific)

PART II

Lessons

Sentence Patterns

Conversations

Example Sentences

Pronunciation of Japanese

I. Japanese syllables

1. The vowels

   tokei (watch), tōkei (statistics), yuki (snow), yūki (courage),
   ojisan (uncle), ojiisan (grandfather),
   obasan (aunt), obāsan (grandmother),
   koko (here), kōkō (filial piety), doro (mud), dōro (road)

2. "n" sounds

   onna (woman), undō (sports), antei (stability),
   shinbun (newspaper), sanpo (walk). bunmei (civilization),
   sankai (three times), kangaemasu (think)

3. Double consonants

   oto (sound), otto (husband),
   shite imasu (be doing), shitte imasu (know),
   hakkiri (clearly), kippu (ticket), motto (more), issai (one year old)

4. Consonants+ya, yu, yo

   hyaku (one hundred), kyaku (guest), ryokō (trip), gyūnyū (milk),
   kyūkō (express), byōki (illness), sangyō (industry), nyūsu (news)

5. "za, zu, zo" and "ja, ju, jo"

   zasshi (magazine), jama (hindrance), zubon (trousers), jūsho (address),
   zōsen (shipbuilding), jōdan (joke), kazu (number), sanjū (thirty),
   kōzō (structure), kōjō (factory)

6. "su" and "tsu"

   isu (chair), itsu (when), kasu (lend), katsu (win),
   Suzuki (Mr. Suzuki), tsuzuki (continuance)

II. Classroom instructions and expressions

1. Let us begin.
2. Let us close the lesson.
3. Let us take a rest.
4. Do you understand?
   — Yes, I understand.
   — No, I don't understand.
5. Altogether, please.
6. Please [say it] once more.
7. Please wait a moment.
8. Please answer [to the question].
9. Fine. Very well. Good.
10. It's no good.

III. Numerals

1 — one
2 — two
3 — three
4 — four
5 — five
6 — six
7 — seven
8 — eight
9 — nine
10 — ten

IV. Greetings

1. Good morning.
2. Good afternoon.
3. Good evening.
4. Good night.
5. Good-bye.

Lesson 1

Sentence Pattern

1. I am Lee.
2. Are you Mr. Tanom?
3. Mr. Tanom is not a Japanese.
4. Mr. Rao is a trainee, too.

Conversation

Tanom : Good morning. I am Tanom of (from) Thailand.
[I] am a trainee of Tokyo-kikai.
I am glad to meet you.

Tanaka : It's very nice meeting you.

Example

1. Are you a trainee?
   — Yes, [I] am a trainee.
   — No, [I] am not a trainee.
2. Are you Mr. Tanom?
   — Yes, [I] am Tanom.
   Are you a teacher?
   — No, [[I] am not a teacher,] [I] am a trainee.
3. Who are you?
   — [I] am Lee.
4. Is Mr. Tanom a Japanese, or a Thai?
   — [Mr. Tanom] is a Thai.
5. Are you an Indian?
   — Yes, I am.
   Is Mr. Lee an Indian, too?
   — No, [he is not,] Mr. Lee is a Chinese.
6. Are you Brazilians?
   — No, [we] are Mexicans.

Lesson 2

Sentence Pattern

1. This is a book.
2. That is my book.
3. That is teacher's.
4. This book is Mr. Tanom's.
5. I am 25 [years old].

Conversation

Lee : Please give me my key.

Kimura : What number ?

Lee : Three-one-eight.

Kimura : Wait a minute, please. Here you are.

Is this your newspaper ?

Lee : Yes, it is. [It's] mine. Thank you very much.

Kimura : Not at all.

Example

1. What is that ?

  — [That] is an ash tray.

2. Whose bag is that ?

  — [This] is Mr. Tanom's bag.

3. Is this dictionary yours ?

  — Yes, [that dictionary] is mine.

  — No, [that dictionary] is not mine.

4. Whose is this pen ?

  — [That pen] is Mr. Tanaka's.

5. Is that dictionary Mr. Tanaka's, or Mr. Rao's ?

  — [That dictionary] is Mr. Rao's.

  Is that Mr. Rao's dictionary, too ?

  — No, [this is not Mr. Rao's,] [that] is Mr. Tanom's.

6. How old are you ?

  — [I] am 34 [years old].

7. What is your speciality ?

  (What are you an expert of ?)

  — [My speciality] is machinery.

Lesson 3

Sentence Pattern

1. The office is over there.
2. The dining hall is that way.
3. This place is a classroom.
4. This is a book on television.
5. This is 1,500 yen.

Conversation

Cortez : Good afternoon.

Rao : Good afternoon.

Cortez : Where/What is your company?

Rao : [My company] is Yokohama-denki.

Cortez : Then, you specialize in radios?

Rao : No, I don't. [My speciality] is TV.

Cortez : Is that so? It is the same as Mr. Lee's, isn't it?

Example

1. Where is the toilet?
   — [The toilet] is there.
2. Which way is the office? (Where is the office?)
   — [The office] is that way. ([The office] is there.)
3. Where is Mr. Rao?
   — [Mr. Rao] is in the office.
4. Where are a match and an ash tray?
   — A match is here and an ash tray is in the lobby.
5. What is this place?
   — [This place] is Kyoto.
6. Where/What is your country?
   — [My country] is India.
7. Where/What is your company?
   — [My company] is Nagoya-jidōsha.
8. What country is that watch made in?
   — [This] is a Swiss-made watch.
9. What is that book about?
   — [This] is a book on automobile.
10. How much is this?
    — [That] is 2,000 yen.

Lesson 4

Sentence Pattern

1. It is ten minutes past one now.
2. I get up at half past six in the morning.
3. I work from 9 o'clock till 5 o'clock.
4. I studied yesterday.

Conversation

Ali   :   Good evening.

Tanaka :   Good evening. This way, please.

             How would you like to have a cup of Japanese tea ?

Ali   :   Yes, [I'd like to]. Thank you.

Tanaka :   From what time do you have a class tomorrow ?

Ali   :   From eight thirty.

Tanaka :   And until what time ?

Ali   :   Till five in the afternoon.

Tanaka :   That's quite tough, isn't it ?

Example

1. What time is it now ?

   — It is five past nine [now].

2. At what time do you go to bed at night ?

   — [I] go to bed at 11 o'clock [at night].

3. Do you work tomorrow ?

   — Yes, [I] work [tomorrow].

   — No, [I] don't work [tomorrow].

4. Did you study yesterday ?

   — Yes, [I] studied [yesterday].

   — No, [I] didn't study [yesterday].

5. From what time and till what time do you take a rest ?

   — [I] take a rest from 12 till half past one.

6. Till what time did you study last night ?

   — [I] studied till eleven [last night].

7. What is the next day of Monday ?

   (What day of the week comes after Monday ?)

   — [The next day of Monday] is Tuesday.

Lesson 5

Sentence Pattern

1. I go to Kyoto. (I will go to Kyoto.)
2. I will go to the factory on April 15th.
3. I will return to my country by airplane.
4. I came [together] with my friends.

Conversation

Tanom : How are you?

Lee   : I'm fine, (thank you).

            How about you?

Tanom : I'm fine, too. (Thank you.)

            Where will you go tomorrow?

Lee   : I won't go anywhere.

Tanom : Well, won't you go to Kyoto with me?

Lee   : That's nice.

Example

1. Where did you go yesterday?
   — [I] went to Kyoto.
   — [I] did not go anywhere.
2. When did you come to Japan?
   — [I] came [to Japan] last month.
   When do you go back to your country?
   — [I] go back [to my country] in September.
3. By what do you go to Kyoto?
   — [I] go [to Kyoto] by Super Express.
4. With whom did Mr. Lee come here?
   — [He] came [here] with Miss Kimura.
5. I came from Ethiopia.
6. [I] go to Nagoya from Osaka by car.
7. Which month and which day (When) is your birthday?
   — It's June 23rd.

Lesson 6

Sentence Pattern

1. I eat meal.
2. I have my practical training in Osaka.
3. Let us listen to a record [together].

Conversation

Cortez : What did you do yesterday?

Slamet : I studied Japanese in the morning. In the afternoon I went to Ginza with my friend.

Cortez : How long does it take from here to Ginza?

Slamet : [It is] 30 minutes by taxi.

Cortez : Is that so?

What did you do at Ginza?

Slamet : I bought this camera at a department store.

Example

1. Do you smoke?

    — Yes, [I] smoke.

    — No, [I] don't smoke.

2. What do you eat every morning?

    — [I] eat bread and eggs.

    — [I] don't eat anything. I drink milk.

3. Where do you take a picture?

    — [I] take [a picture] in the garden.

4. What did you do last night?

    — [I] watched television in the dining hall.

    What are you going to do tomorrow?

    — [I] am going to Kyoto.

5. Don't we have tea together?

    — Yes, let's drink [some].

Lesson 7

Sentence Pattern

1. Japanese people eat meals with chopsticks.
2. I [will] write a report in Japanese.
3. I will telephone my friend.
4. I learned Japanese from Mr. Tanaka.

Conversation

Slamet : Excuse me.

Tanaka : Yes. What can I do for you?

Slamet : How much does this baggage cost by airmail?

Tanaka : Where do you send it?

Slamet : To Jakarta in Indonesia.

Tanaka : It is 1 kg.

It costs 600 yen.

Slamet : Will [it] arrive [there] next week?

Tanaka : Yes, sure.

Slamet : Thank you.

Example

1. With what do you repair cars?
   — [I] repair [cars] with screw drivers and spanners.
2. What is "Good night" in Japanese?
   — ["Good night"] is "Oyasuminasai" [in Japanese].
3. To whom do you give the book?
   — [I] give [this book] to Mr. Tanom.
4. What did you receive (get) from Mr. Slamet?
   — [I] received (got) a watch [from Mr. Slamet].
5. Have you read this book?
   — Yes, [I] have read [it] already.
   — No, [I] have not read [it] yet.

Lesson 8

Sentence Pattern

1. Cherryblossoms are beautiful flowers.
2. Cherryblossoms are beautiful.
3. Cherryblossoms are not beautiful.
4. This is a big bag.
5. This is big.
6. This is not big.

Conversation

Ali   :   Hi, I'm home.

Kimura :   Nice to see you back.

              Where did you go?

Ali   :   I visited Mr. Tanom's home.

Kimura :   Oh, did you.

              What does his house look like?

Ali   :   [It's] a small, but a new house.

              I met Mr. Tanom's wife.

Kimura :   What type of person is Mrs. Tanom?

Ali   :   She's pretty, and very kind.

Example

1. Is Mr. Tanaka kind?
   - Yes, [he] is kind.
   - No, [he] is not kind.
2. Is the camera good?
   - Yes, [it] is very good.
   - No, [it] is not so good.
3. What kind of city is Nara? (What is Nara like?)
   - [It] is a quiet city.
4. How do you like Japanese food?
   - [It] is tasty.
5. Is it cold or hot in your country now?
   - [It] is very hot.
6. Is the examination difficult?
   - No, [it] is not difficult, [it] is easy.
7. Whose is that red bag?
   - [It] is Mr. Tanaka's.

Lesson 9

Sentence Pattern

1. I like apples.
2. Miss Arora is good at dancing.
3. I do not understand Chinese characters.
4. I have children.

Conversation

Tanaka : What's the matter with you?

Rao : I've caught cold, and I have a slight headache.

Tanaka : Did you go to a hospital? (Have you gone to a hospital?)

Rao : No, I won't go. (No, I haven't.)

Tanaka : Why not?

Rao : Because I don't like injection.

Tanaka : Shall I give you medicine, then?

Rao : Yes, please. (Thank you.)

Example

1. Do you like beer?
    — Yes, I like [it].
    — No, I don't like [it]. ([I] dislike [it].)
2. What kind of sports do you like?
    — I like tennis.
3. Is Mr. Tanom good or poor at singing?
    — [He] is good [at it].
4. Do you know how to use a typewriter?
    — Yes, I know well.
    — No, I don't know at all.
5. How much money do you have?
    — I have just 100 yen.
6. As I have a stomachache, I will go to bed in my room.
7. Why did you absent yourself from company?
    — Because I had a slight fever.

Lesson 10

Sentence Pattern

1. There is a trainee in the classroom. /There are trainees in the classroom.
2. There is a book on the desk. /There are books on the desk.
3. Mr. Tanaka is in the office.
4. The bank is [located] next to the post office.
5. Near the Center, there are a department store, a restaurant, a hospital, [and so on].

Conversation

Ali : Is Mr. Tanaka [still] in the office?

Kimura : He's gone home already.

Ali : Where is Mr. Tanaka's house?

Kimura : There's a flower-shop in front of the station, you know? His house is next to the flower-shop.

Ali : I see. Well, I [think I will] go [there] now.

Kimura : See you later. (Have a nice time.)

Ali : I'll see you later.

Example

1. Who is there?
   — There is a trainee. /There are trainees.
   — There is nobody.
2. What is there in the box?
   — There are bolts and nuts.
   — There is nothing.
3. Where is Mr. Tanaka?
   — [He] is in the lobby.
4. Where is the department store?
   — [It] is near the station.
5. Where is the switch?
   — [It] is to the right of the door.
6. Nagoya is between Tokyo and Osaka.
7. The office is to the left of the lobby on the second floor.

Lesson 11

Sentence Pattern

1. There is one apple.
2. There are two trainees.
3. Mr. Rao takes the practical training for 6 months in Japan.
4. I wash my clothes once a week.

Conversation

Cortez : How many people are there in this factory?

Factory personnel : About 400 people.

Cortez : How many machines are there?

Factory personnel : There are about 30.

Cortez : Are they foreign-made?

Factory personnel : No, all are made in Japan.

Cortez : How many cameras do [you] make (produce) a day?

Factory personnel : It's 100.

Example

1. How many classrooms are there in the Center?
   — There are three.
2. How many trainees are there at your company?
   — There are six.
3. How many children do you have?
   — [I] have two.
4. For how many months do trainees take practical training in Japan?
   — [They] take [practical training] for about six months.
5. How long are you going to stay in Japan? /How long have you been in Japan?
   — One year.
6. How many times a week do you write a letter?
   — [I] write twice.
7. These apples, how much are they a piece?
   — 50 yen.
   Give me three, then.
   — [They are] 150 yen in all.
8. Please give me three fifteen-yen stamps.
9. They produce 1,400 automobiles a day in this factory.

— 62 —

Lesson 12

Sentence Pattern

1. Tokyo is bigger than Osaka.
2. [I] like bananas best of all the fruits.
3. [It] was rainy yesterday. (It rained yesterday.)
4. [It] was cold the day before yesterday.

Conversation

Kimura : Very nice weather, isn't it ?

How are you getting along with your work ?

Ali   : Well, I'm always busy. Sometimes I work even at night.

Kimura : When are you usually free (least busy) ?

Ali   : Well . . . I'm free on Saturday evenings.

Kimura : Won't you come to my home?

Ali   : Yes, [I will]. Around what time is most convenient for you ?

Kimura : Around 5 o'clock is all right [for me].

Example

1. Which is more difficult, English or Japanese ?
   — English is more difficult.
   — Both are difficult.
2. Which is nearest, Thailand, India or Iran ?
   — Thailand is nearest.
3. Who is the youngest, Mr. Tanom, Mr. Lee or Mr. Rao ?
   — Mr. Rao is the youngest.
4. Which runs fastest, a ship, an airplane or a train ?
   — An airplane runs fastest.
5. What do you like best among sports ?
   — I like pingpong best.
6. Was it holiday yesterday ?
   — Yes, [it] was holiday.
   — No, [it] was not holiday.
7. Was the tour enjoyable ?   (Did you enjoy your tour ?)
   — Yes, [it] was enjoyable.
   How was the weather ?
   — [It] was not so good.

Lesson 13

Sentence Pattern

1. I want a camera.
2. I want to see a movie.
3. I go to the dining hall to eat meal.
4. I came to Japan to take practical training in electricity.

Conversation

Rao : Where are you going?

Lee : I'm going to a department store to buy a radio set.

Rao : I also want a radio set.

Lee : Let's go together, then.

. . . .

Lee : Oh, I am tired.

Rao : I am thirsty.

[We] want to have a glass of beer, don't we?

Lee : Shall we go into that restaurant?

Rao : Yes, let's do so.

Example

1. What do you want?
   — [I] want a car.
   — [I] don't want anything.
2. What kind of camera do you want?
   — [I] want a small camera.
3. What do you want to read?
   — [I] want to read a Thai newspaper.
   — [I] don't want to read anything.
4. What do you want to do?
   — [I] want to do a sightseeing in Kyoto.
5. What do you want to drink?
   — Anything is all right.
6. Where do you go to buy souvenirs?
   — [I] go to a department store to buy [them].
7. What do you go to Tokyo for?
   — [I] go [to Tokyo] to see my friend.
8. For what study have you come to Japan?
   — [I] have come [to Japan] for the study of elevator.
9. Where do you want to go [to enjoy yourself]?
   — [I] want to go to Shinjuku.

Lesson 14

Sentence Pattern

1. Please lend me a dictionary.
2. Mr. Lee is smoking now.

Conversation

Store attendant	:	Welcome, sir.
Lee	:	Show me tape recorders.
Store attendant	:	There are various kinds. What kind of tape recorder do you want ?
Lee	:	Give me a small one.
Store attendant	:	How about this cassette ?
Lee	:	How much is that ?
Store attendant	:	It's 20,000 yen.
Lee	:	Let me take it. (Give me that one.)

Example

1. Please say it more slowly.
2. Excuse me, but please pass me the salt.
   — Here you are.
3. What is Mr. Slamet doing now ?
   — [He] is listening to the music in his room.
4. We have little time [left], so please hurry up.
   — Just a moment. Mr. Lee has not come yet.
   What is Mr. Lee doing ?
   — [He] is talking with a man from the company in the lobby.
5. It is raining. Shall I call a taxi ?
   — Yes, please call [one].

Lesson 15

Sentence Pattern

1. You may use this tape recorder.
2. I have a good camera.

Conversation

Rao   : Mr. Ali, do you know that lady?

Ali   : No, I don't know [her]. Who's she?

Rao   : [She] is Ms. Suzuki. She lives near the Center.

Ali   : A pretty lady, isn't she? Is she single?

Rao   : No, she's already married.

Example

1. Okay?

    — Yes, okay.

    — No, it's not good.

2. Is it all right if [I] go home now? (May I go back now?)

    — Yes, you may go home.

    — No, it is not good [if [you] go home now].   (No, you must not [go home].)

3. Do you have an umbrella?

    — No, I don't.

    Then shall I lend you mine?

    — Yes, please lend me.

4. Where do you live?

    — [I] live in Kenshu Center.

    Then, do you know Mr. Rao from India?

    — Yes, I know.

    — No, I don't know.

5. What does your company make?

    — [It] makes television sets.

6. Where do they sell postage stamps, envelopes and so on?

    — They sell at the information desk.

7. It has become dark. Shall I put on the light?

    — Yes, please put it on.

Lesson 16

Sentence Pattern

1. I got up in the morning, had breakfast, and came to the classroom.
2. This apple is big and delicious.
3. You are an Indian, and I am a Japanese.
4. After the work was over, [we] saw the movies.

Conversation

Slamet : Excuse me. Please lend me a record player for a while.

Tanaka : Sure. This one is light and reproduces good sound.

Slamet : May I use it till tomorrow?

Tanaka : No, it's not OK for me.

I need the player, too.

Slamet : Then, I'll come to return it later on.

Example

1. Did you go to Tokyo yesterday?

    — Yes, [I] went immediately after the lecture was over.

    What did you do after going to Tokyo?

    — [I] went to Ginza, met my friend, and [we] drank beer together.

2. Who (what) is that person?

    — [He] is Mr. Rao.

    [He] is an Indian, and a trainee of Osaka-kagaku.

3. What type of person is Miss Arora?

    — [She] is young, pretty and intelligent.

4. What do you do after the lecture is over?

    — [I] go to my room and take a rest.

Lesson 17

Sentence Pattern

1. Do not forget me.
2. Trainees must study everyday.
3. You need not pay money now.

Conversation

Lee   :   Excuse me. Is Mr. Tanaka in?

Tanaka :   Hello, Mr. Lee! I haven't seen you for a long time. Are you all right now?

Lee   :   Yes, I'm all right now, so please don't worry.

Tanaka :   Well, I'm glad to hear that.

. . . .

Lee   :   It's already nine o'clock. I must be going home.

Tanaka :   Well, take care of yourself.

Lee   :   I will. Thank you very much.

Example

1. Please don't put sugar in [my] coffee.
2. Do [we] have to speak Japanese in the factory?
   — Yes, [we] have to speak [it].
   — No, [we] don't have to speak [it].
   (It is all right even if [we] don't speak [it].)
3. By what time do you have to return to the Center?
   — [I] have to return by 8 o'clock.
4. Must [we] (Do [we] have to) take off [our] shoes at the Center?
   — No, [we] need not take them off.
5. Please don't touch this switch.
   — Why is it?
   Because [it's] dangerous.
   — I see. I'll be careful.

Lesson 18

Sentence Pattern

1. I can drive a car.
2. I can speak Japanese a little.
3. Please telephone me before you come here.

Conversation

Cortez : Hello. Is Mr. Kato in ? (Can I speak to Mr. Kato ?)

Mrs. Kato : He is not here now. Who is this, please ?

Cortez : I'm Cortez from Mexico. Tomorrow I am going back to my country. Before leaving, I want to see Mr. Kato.

Mrs. Kato : My husband went on a trip yesterday.

Cortez : Oh, he did ? That's too bad. Please give my best regards to him.

Mrs. Kato : Certainly. Best of luck.

Example

1. Can you speak Japanese ?   (Do you understand Japanese ?)
   — Yes, I can, a little.
2. Can you repair a television ?
   — No, I can't [repair].
3. What do you do before [you] go to bed ?
   — I take a shower.
4. When did you get married ?
   — I got married shortly before I came to Japan.
5. Before you came to Japan, did you study Japanese ?
   — No, I did not study [it] at all.
   Then, when did you start studying ?
   — I started immediately after I came to Japan.

Lesson 19

Sentence Pattern

1. I have seen Mt. Fuji before.
2. As the bus is slow, you had better go by train.
3. As you are ill, you had better not go outside.
4. Won't you play pingpong [with me] after you have eaten?

Conversation

Tanom : Excuse me, aren't you Mr. Kato?

Katō : I beg your pardon. May I ask your name?

Tanom : I'm Tanom from Thailand. I met you once in Bangkok three years ago.

Katō : Oh, you are Mr. Tanom! I'm sorry [I could not recognize you].

Tanom : No, that's all right. This is Mr. Lee.

　　　　 He is taking practical training at the same company as mine.

Lee : I'm glad to meet you.

Katō : It's nice to meet you.

Example

1. Have you ever seen snow?

　　 — Yes, I have [seen it].

　　 — No, I have not [seen it].

2. Have you ever been to Ginza?

　　 — Yes, I have [been there] once.

3. Would it be better for me to take medicine?

　　 (Should I take medicine?)

　　 — Yes, you had better take [it].

　　 (Yes, you should take [some].)

　　 — No, you had better not take [it].

4. After having lunch, what are you going to do?

　　 — I'm going to take a walk in the park.

5. After the orientation course, [I will] go to the factory in Hiroshima.

6. You had better not buy [anything] at Ginza, because it is expensive.

　　 — Then, where should I buy [it] cheaper?

　　 — Ueno or Asakusa is better. Have you ever been there?

　　 — No, I've never been there.

Lesson 20

Sentence Pattern

Refer to the text for the Polite form and the Plain form.

Conversation (the plain style of conversation of lesson 5)

Tanom : How are you?

Lee   : I'm okay, [thank you].

            How about you?

Tanom : I'm okay, too. Where are you going tomorrow?

Lee   : I'm not going anywhere.

Tanom : Then, would you like to go to Kyoto with me?

Lee   : That's nice.

Example

1. Mr. Tanaka is good at playing the piano.
2. I like fruits.
3. I want a camera now.
4. I want to return to my country soon.
5. Mr. Lee is smoking now.
6. You may use this tape recorder.
7. I have a good camera.
8. I don't know Mr. Rao's address.
9. Trainees have to study everyday.
10. You do not have to pay money now.
11. I can drive a car.
12. I cannot speak French.
13. I have seen Mt. Fuji before.
14. I never rode on the Super Express.
15. As the bus is slow, you had better go by train.

Lesson 21

Sentence Pattern

1. I think that there will be a Japanese language test tomorrow.
2. The teacher said, "Please come to the office."
3. It will probably rain tomorrow. (...might rain...)
4. Mr. Lee will probably come tomorrow. (...might come...)

Conversation

Tanaka : What do you think about Japan?

Lee : Well, let me see. I think it's a beautiful country, but I don't know much yet.

Tanaka : Mr. Tanom says things are expensive in Japan.

Lee : I think so, too.

Tanaka : Especially food is expensive, don't you think so?

Lee : That's true.

　　　　But electric appliances are far cheaper here than in my country.

Tanaka : Are you going to buy some to take back home?

Lee : Yes, I want to do so.

Example

1. What do you think about Japanese people?
   — [I] think that [they] are kind.
   — [I] think that [they] are not so kind.
2. How is this examination? (How do you find this examination?)
   — [I] think that [it] is difficult.
   — [I] think that [it] is not so difficult.
3. How was the examination of this morning?
   — [I] think that [it] was very difficult.
   — [I] think that [it] was not so difficult.
4. Will Mr. Tanom come tomorrow?
   — Yes, [I] think that [he] will come.
   — No, [I] think that [he] will not come.
5. Was there a party yesterday?
   — Yes, [I] think that there was.
   — No, [I] think that there was not.
6. What did the teacher say?
   — [He] said that [we] may go back.
7. Can that person speak Japanese?
   — Probably he can.
8. Japanese language is interesting, don't you think?
   — Yes, it's interesting.

Lesson 22

Sentence Pattern

1. When you go out of the room, please turn off the light.
2. When it rains, I stay at home.
3. Having no money, we will be in trouble.
4. Turning to the right, you see a department store.

Conversation

Tanaka : When you go to the factory, how do you usually go ?

Ali : I get on a train at Komagome, and change trains at Shinagawa. Then I get off the train at Kawasaki.

Tanaka : Tomorrow I want to visit your factory, so show me the way.

Ali : You walk straight from the station for about 100 meters, and there's a crossing.

Tanaka : Crossing, yes. Shall I cross it ?

Ali : No. Turn to the left.

You go for 50 meters and you'll find a bridge.

Cross the bridge and there's the factory on the right.

Tanaka : Thanks. I understood very well.

Example

1. When I'm busy, please help me.
2. When you are free, please come and see me.
3. Let's be (You should be) careful about cars, when you walk along the street.
4. When I went to Tokyo, I bought these shoes.
5. When you were a child, where did you live ?
   — [I] lived in Osaka.
6. If you have no money, what would you do ?
   — [I] borrow [some] from my friend.
7. When [your] friend gets married, what do [you] say [to him or her] ?
   — [We] say, "Omedetō gozaimasu."
8. [You] need a passport when [you] do shopping, go on a trip [and things like that].
9. When we drink 'sake', we feel happy.
10. If [you] do not study harder, [you'll] be in trouble.

Lesson 23

Sentence Pattern

1. The person who came yesterday is a friend of Miss Kimura.
2. This is the picture that I took.
3. Please show me the camera which you bought last week.
4. I have no time to write a letter.

Conversation

Tanaka : Are there any questions about the study tour?

Slamet : The factory we are going to visit in Nagoya, what kind of a factory is it?

Tanaka : It's the factory manufacturing automobiles. It's the biggest maker in Japan.

Slamet : What is the place we'll go after Nagoya?

Tanaka : Hiroshima.

Here we see the Peace Memorial Park and a factory of machines.

Slamet : I have a friend in Hiroshima. Will there be any time to see him?

Tanaka : Well, I don't think we'll have much time. Any other questions?

Slamet : No more.

Example

1. Who is the person that came to the Center yesterday?
   — [He] is a man from my company.
2. Who is the person that is singing a song over there?
   — [He] is Mr. Tanom.
3. What is your favorite sport?
   — [It] is soccer.
4. The movie which I saw yesterday was interesting.
5. By whom was this picture taken?
   — This is a picture which Mr. Tanaka took.
   Where was this picture taken?
   — This is a picture taken in Kyoto.
   When was this picture taken?
   — This is a picture taken last Sunday.
6. Do you know where they sell dictionaries?
   — Yes, I know.
7. Which was the most interesting of all the lectures that you heard (attended)?

Lesson 24

Sentence Pattern

1. It is difficult to speak Japanese.
2. My hobby is painting pictures.
3. I like to listen to jazz.
4. [Do you] know that he went home?

Conversation

Kimura : How long have you studied the Japanese language?

Rao : Four weeks.

Kimura : Is that true? You speak so well!

Is it difficult to speak Japanese?

Rao : Yes, it is difficult.

Kimura : Can you read Hiragana and Katakana?

Rao : No, not yet.

Now I'm studying [Japanese] in Roman letters.

I want to learn how to write [Hiragana and Katakana] from now.

Kimura : Do you?

Try your best. (Good luck.)

Example

1. Smoking is harmful to health.
2. What is your hobby?
   — [My hobbies] are listening to the music, playing the guitar, and so on.
3. What sort of sports do you like?
   — Baseball.
   Do you play it yourself?
   — No, I like to watch.
4. Do [you] know that there would be no test tomorrow?
   — No, [I] don't know.
5. Did [you] hear that Mrs. Rao would come next week?
   — Yes, [I] heard.

Lesson 25

Sentence Pattern

1. If [you] talk slowly, [I] understand.
2. If [you] do not understand, please ask me.
3. If [I] had money, [I] would like to go to India.
4. Even if it rains, [I] will go.
5. I searched everywhere, but still I can't find it.

Conversation

Lee : How do you operate this machine?

Katō : First, turn on the switch, and then push this button, and it will work.

Lee : Quite simple, isn't it?

Katō : Yes. But if the red light is on, it means there's something wrong with the machine. So, stop it right away.

Lee : When it doesn't work, what should I do?

Katō : Check it well with the tester.

If you still can't find the cause, please call for me.

Example

1. Whom do [you] like to meet when you go to Yokohama?
   — [I] want to see Mr. Slamet.
2. If it rains tomorrow, what will [you] do?
   — [I] will stay at home all day.
3. Won't [you] go with me this Sunday?
   — If [I] am free, [I] will go, but if [I] am busy, [I] will not go.
4. Where should [I] change money?
   — [You] should change [it] at the bank.
5. How should [I] go to the bank?
   — Go straight along this street.
6. [I] want to borrow some books; what should [I] do?
   — Please ask the person at the information.
7. If [it] were cheap, would [you] buy it?
   — Yes, if [it] were cheap, [I] would buy it.
   — No, even if [it] were cheap, [I] will not buy [it].
8. Even if it rains, are you going?
   — Yes, I will go, even if it rains.
   — No, I won't go, if it rains.

Lesson 26

Sentence Pattern

1. I can speak Thai and Japanese.
2. [I] could not sleep well last night.
3. The sea can be seen from my room. [I can see the sea from my room.]
4. [I] hear a noise of cars.

Conversation

Cortez : Can I get to Shin-Osaka by one o'clock ?

Tanaka : Sure, you can reach there in 20 minutes from here.

Cortez : Can I buy the ticket right away ?

Tanaka : We can buy it any time.

Cortez : Can I have a meal in Shinkansen ?

Tanaka : Yes, you can, because there's a buffet.

Cortez : I see.

Tanaka : There's also a telephone service. You can ring up Tokyo, Osaka, and so on.

Cortez : That's convenient.

Example

1. Can you read Chinese characters ?
   — Yes, [I] can read [them] a little.
   — No, [I] can't read [them] at all.
2. How well can you swim ?
   — [I] can swim about 500 meters.
3. Can you get up at six tomorrow ?
   — Yes, [I] think [I] can.
   — No, [I] don't think [I] can.
4. Can you come again tomorrow ?
   — Yes, [I] can come.
   — No, [I] cannot come.
5. Can you repair the television set ?
   — No, [I] cannot.
6. Can you remember Japanese names ?
   — No, [they are] difficult, and [I] can't remember.
7. This water is drinkable.
8. This fish is not edible.
9. Dinner is ready.
10. A new road has been constructed.

Lesson 27

Sentence Pattern

1. I showed the pictures to Miss. Kimura.
2. Mr. Tanom [kindly] showed me the pictures.
3. I had Mr. Tanom show the pictures for me.
4. Won't you please tell me [your] address ?
5. The professor has gone home already.
6. Come in, please.
7. Mr. Tanaka will come here at nine o'clock tomorrow.
8. Mr. Kimura said so.

Conversation

Tanaka : Hello, Mr. Tanom. I haven't seen you for a long time.
Have a seat. When did you come here ?

Tanom : Last night.

Tanaka : Is that so ? I suppose you got very tired.
Could you sleep well last night ?

Tanom : Yes, I slept till ten o'clock this morning. I'm going to Tokyo now.

Tanaka : It's almost twelve o'clock. Won't you have lunch here ?

Tanom : Yes, thank you very much.

Example

1. Shall I lend you my camera ?
   — Yes, please.
2. From whom did you get the help ?
   — Mr. Lee kindly helped me.
3. Won't you please close the curtain ?
4. Please sit down.
5. Mr. Cortez, please come to the information.
6. How long did you wait ?
   — I waited for about 20 minutes.
7. Are you coming here tomorrow ?
   — Yes, I am coming.
8. Did you go to Indonesia last month ?
   — Yes, I did.
9. Will you be in the Center tomorrow ?
   — No, I won't be.
10. What did the professor say ?
    — The professor said, "Best regards to everyone."

Lesson 28

— Particles —

1. **wa**   Lesson
    1) I am Lee.   (1)

2. **no**
    A: 1) This is my book.   (2)
        2) I am a trainee of Tokyo-kikai.   (3)
        3) This is a Japan-made watch.   (3)
        4) This is a book on television.   (3)
    B: 1) This is mine.   (2)
        2) Give me the small one.   (14)

3. **o**
    1) [I] eat meal.   (6)
    2) [I] take a day off from my company.   (9)
    3) [I] go out of the room.   (13)
    4) [I] get off a train.   (16)
    5) [I] walk across the bridge.   (22)

4. **ga**
    A: 1) I have children.   (9)
        2) I like bananas.   (9)
        3) I don't like fish.   (9)
        4) Mr. Lee is good at pingpong.   (9)
        5) I am poor at dancing.   (9)
        6) I understand Japanese.   (9)
        7) I want a camera.   (13)
        8) I need money.   (16)
        9) I can speak Japanese.   (18)
       10) I want to see the movies.   (13)
       11) Miss Arora is clever.   (16)
    B: 1) There is a trainee (There are trainees) in the classroom.   (10)
        2) There is a desk (There are desks) in the classroom.   (10)
    C: 1) Mr. Rao is the youngest.   (12)
        2) It is raining.   (14)
    D: 1) My room is small but clean.   (8)
        2) There are many models. What kind of tape recorder do you want ? (14)

— 79 —

E: 1) When your friend is getting married, what do you say to him ? (22)

2) This is the photo which I took. (23)

5. **ni**

1) [I] get up at six every morning. (4)

2) [I] write a letter to my friend. (7)

3) [I] learned Japanese from Mr. Tanaka. (7)

4) [I] meet my friend. (8)

5) Here is a book. (10)

6) [I] wash my clothes once a week. (11)

7) [I] go to the dining hall to eat. (13)

8) Let's get into that restaurant. (13)

9) Mr. Lee becomes a teacher. (15)

10) [I] get on a train. (16)

6. **e**

1) [I] go to Yokohama. (5)

7. **de**

1) [I] came by airplane. (5)

2) [I] take photos in the garden. (6)

3) [I] write letters with a pen. (7)

4) [I] write reports in Japanese. (7)

8. **to**

A: 1) Where are the matches and the ash tray? (3)

B: 1) [I] go with my friend. (5)

9. **ya — nado**

1) Here are books, notebooks, pencils, and so on. (10)

10. **kara — made**

1) [I] take a rest from 12 o'clock till 1 o'clock. (4)

2) [I] go from Tokyo to Osaka by Shinkansen train. (5)

11. **kara**

A: 1) As I have a stomachache, I will go to bed in my room. (9)

12. **ka**

A: 1) Are you Mr. Tanom? (1)

B: 1) Ueno or Asakusa would be nice. (19)

13. **yori**

1) Tokyo is larger than Osaka. (12)

14. **mo**

  A: 1) He is a trainee. And I am a trainee, too.   (1)

  B: 1) [I] won't go anywhere.   (5)

       2) [I] don't eat anything.   (6)

       3) No one is here.   (10)

15. **demo**

       1) Anything is all right. (Anything will do.)   (13)

16. **ne**

       1) It's the same as Mr. Lee, isn't it?   (3)

17. **yo**

       1) She is Suzuki. (Here is Suzuki.)   (15)

Lesson 29

— Verb etc.+Conjugation Patterns —

			Lesson
1.	**[masu]-form**+ tai desu	[I] want to drink.	(13)
2.	**[masu]-form**+ ni ikimasu	[I] go to drink.	(13)
3.	o+**[masu]-form**+ ni narimasu	He drinks. (Honorific)	(27)
4.	o+**[masu]-form**+ kudasai	Please drink. (Honorific)	(27)
5.	**te-form** + kudasai	Please write.	(14)
6.	**te-form** + imasu	[I] am writing.	(14)
7.	**te-form** + mo ii desu	You may write.	(15)
8.	**te-form** + kara, —	After writing, [I] sleep.	(16)
9.	**te-form** + mo, —	Even if you write, I don't understand (it).	(25)
10.	**te-form** + agemasu	I write for you.	(27)
11.	**te-form** + kudasaimasu	[He] writes for me.	(27)
12.	**te-form** + moraimasu	I have him write for me.	(27)
13.	**[nai]-form** + nai de kudasai	Please don't go.	(17)
14.	**[nai]-form** + nakereba narimasen	I have to go. (I must go.)	(17)
15.	**[nai]-form** + nakute mo ii desu	You need not go. (You don't have to go.)	(17)
16.	**dictionary-form** + koto ga dekimasu	[I] can eat (it).	(18)
17.	**dictionary-form** + mae ni, —	Before eating, [I] wash.	(18)
18.	**dictionary-form** / **nai-form** } + to, —	If you eat, you will feel better. / If you don't eat, you will get sick.	(22)
19.	**dictionary-form** + koto ga suki desu	[I] like eating.	(24)
20.	**ta-form** + koto ga arimasu	[I] have read it before.	(19)
21.	**ta-form** / **nai-form** } + hō ga ii desu	You had better read it. / You had better not read it.	(19)
22.	**ta-form** + ato de, —	After reading, [I] sleep.	(19)
23.	**plain-form** + to omoimasu	I think that —	(21)

24. **verb** / **i-adjective** } plain-form

noun, na-adjective { .... / dewa nai / datta / dewa nakatta } + { deshō — It will — (21) / kamo shiremasen — It may — (21) }

— 82 —

25. **verb**
    i-adjective } **plain-form**

    noun {
- no
- dewa nai
- datta
- dewa nakatta

    na-adjective {
- na
- dewa nai
- datta
- dewa nakatta

+ {
toki, —	(at) the time when —	(22)
hito, etc. **(noun)**	the person who —	(23)
koto	the fact that —	(24)

26. **plain-form ·past** + ra, —   If —   (25)

Lesson 30

— The Usages of Verbs and Adjectives —

1. quick (**i-adjective**) .... quickly, early (**adverb**)

   example: quick .... walk quickly

   slow .... walk slowly

   good, well .... understand well

   busy .... to work busily (actively)

2. quiet (**na-adjective**) .... quietly (**adverb**)

   example: quiet .... speak quietly

   clean .... clean up

   kind .... teach kindly

   cheerful .... play cheerfully

3. to take a rest (**verb**) .... a rest (**noun**)

   example: to take a rest ...... Today is a holiday (a day-off)

   to go .... That train is bound for Tokyo.

   to speak .... [I] listened to what the teacher said.

   to begin .... Please read from the beginning.

   to finish .... [I] go home at the end of this month.

4. heavy (**i-adjective**) .... weight (**noun**)

   example: heavy .... The weight of this bag is 5 kg.

   high .... The height of Tokyo Tower is 333 m.

   long .... What is the length of the pencil?

   fast .... The speed of Shinkansen is 163 km/h.

5. to read (**verb**) .... how to read (**noun**)

   example: to read .... [I] don't know how to read Kanji.

   to make .... Do you know how to cook the Indian dish?

   to write .... Please show me how to write a letter.

   to use .... Do you know how to use a typewriter (how to type)?

6. big (**i-adjective**) .... become big

   quiet (**na-adjective**) .... become quiet

   12 o'clock (**noun**) .... become 12 o'clock

   example: The child grew bigger and bigger.

   When the party was over, it became quiet.

   I became 20 years old last month.

7. fast **(i-adjective)** ....make it fast, do . . . fast

   quiet **(na-adjective)** ....be quiet

   tomorrow **(noun)** ....do it tomorrow

    example: As I have no time, please do it quickly.

             As I am studying now, please be quiet.

             As I am busy today, let's do it tomorrow.

PART III

Appendices

APPENDIX 1

sūji　すうじ　*numerals*

1	ichi	いち		200	ni-hyaku	にひゃく
2	ni	に		300	san-byaku	さんびゃく
3	san	さん		400	yon-hyaku	よんひゃく
4	shi, yon	し，よん		500	go-hyaku	ごひゃく
5	go	ご		600	rop-pyaku	ろっぴゃく
6	roku	ろく		700	nana-hyaku	ななひゃく
7	shichi, nana	しち，なな		800	hap-pyaku	はっぴゃく
8	hachi	はち		900	kyū-hyaku	きゅうひゃく
9	ku, kyū	く，きゅう		1,000	sen	せん
10	jū	じゅう		2,000	ni-sen	にせん
11	jū-ichi	じゅういち		3,000	san-zen	さんぜん
12	jū-ni	じゅうに		4,000	yon-sen	よんせん
13	jū-san	じゅうさん		5,000	go-sen	ごせん
14	jū-yon	じゅうよん		6,000	roku-sen	ろくせん
15	jū-go	じゅうご		7,000	nana-sen	ななせん
16	jū-roku	じゅうろく		8,000	has-sen	はっせん
17	jū-nana	じゅうなな		9,000	kyū-sen	きゅうせん
18	jū-hachi	じゅうはち				
19	jū-kyū	じゅうきゅう		10,000	ichi-man	いちまん
20	ni-jū	にじゅう		100,000	jū-man	じゅうまん
21	ni-jū-ichi	にじゅういち		1,000,000	hyaku-man	ひゃくまん
30	san-jū	さんじゅう		10,000,000	sen-man	せんまん
40	yon-jū	よんじゅう		100,000,000	ichi-oku	いちおく
50	go-jū	ごじゅう		0.5	rei-ten-go	れいてんご
60	roku-jū	ろくじゅう		0.76	rei-ten-nana-roku	
70	nana-jū	ななじゅう				れいてんななろく
80	hachi-jū	はちじゅう		$\frac{1}{2}$	ni-bun no ichi	にぶんのいち
90	kyū-jū	きゅうじゅう		$\frac{3}{4}$	yon-bun no san	よんぶんのさん
100	hyaku	ひゃく				

hi ひ *day*	ototoi おととい *the day before yesterday*	kinō きのう *yesterday*	kyō きょう *today*
asa あさ *morning*	ototoi no asa おとといの あさ *the morning before last*	kinō no asa きのうの あさ *yesterday morning*	kesa けさ *this morning*
ban ばん *evening, night*	ototoi no ban おとといの ばん *the night before last*	kinō no ban きのうの ばん *last night*	konban こんばん *tonight*
shū しゅう *week*	ni-shūkan mae (sen-sen-shū) にしゅうかんまえ （せんせんしゅう） *the week before last*	sen-shū せんしゅう *last week*	kon-shū こんしゅう *this week*
tsuki つき *month*	ni-kagetsu mae (sen-sen-getsu) にかげつまえ （せんせんげつ） *the month before last*	sen-getsu せんげつ *last month*	kon-getsu こんげつ *this month*
toshi とし *year*	ototoshi おととし *the year before last*	kyonen きょねん *last year*	kotoshi ことし *this year*

yōbi ようび

nichi-yōbi にちようび *Sunday*	getsu-yōbi げつようび *Monday*	ka-yōbi かようび *Tuesday*	sui-yōbi すいようび *Wednesday*

time expression

ashita あした *tomorrow*	**asatte** あさって *the day after tomorrow*	**mai-nichi** まいにち *everyday*
ashita no asa あしたの あさ *tomorrow morning*	**asatte no asa** あさっての あさ *the morning after next*	**mai-asa** まいあさ *every morning*
ashita no ban あしたの ばん *tomorrow evening*	**asatte no ban** あさっての ばん *the evening after next*	**mai-ban** まいばん *every evening*
rai-shū らいしゅう *next week*	**sa-rai-shū** さらいしゅう *the week after next*	**mai-shū** まいしゅう *every week*
rai-getsu らいげつ *next month*	**sa-rai-getsu** さらいげつ *the month after next*	**mai-tsuki** まいつき *every month*
rai-nen らいねん *next year*	**sa-rai-nen** さらいねん *the year after next*	**mai-nen** まいねん *every year*

days of the week

moku-yōbi もくようび *Thursday*	**kin-yōbi** きんようび *Friday*	**do-yōbi** どようび *Saturday*	**nan-yōbi** なんようび *what day of the week*

jikoku じこく *telling time*

ji じ o'clock		fun ふん *minute*		tsuki つき	
1	ichi-ji いちじ *one o'clock*	1	ip-pun いっぷん *one minute*	1	ichi-gatsu いちがつ
2	ni-ji にじ	2	ni-fun にふん	2	ni-gatsu にがつ
3	san-ji さんじ	3	san-pun さんぷん	3	san-gatsu さんがつ
4	yo-ji よじ	4	yon-pun よんぷん	4	shi-gatsu しがつ
5	go-ji ごじ	5	go-fun ごふん	5	go-gatsu ごがつ
6	roku-ji ろくじ	6	rop-pun ろっぷん	6	roku-gatsu ろくがつ
7	shichi-ji しちじ	7	nana-fun ななふん	7	shichi-gatsu しちがつ
8	hachi-ji はちじ	8	hap-pun, hachi-fun はっぷん, はちふん	8	hachi-gatsu はちがつ
9	ku-ji くじ	9	kyū-fun きゅうふん	9	ku-gatsu くがつ
10	jū-ji じゅうじ	10	jup-pun じゅっぷん	10	jū-gatsu じゅうがつ
11	jūichi-ji じゅういちじ	11	jūip-pun じゅういっぷん	11	jūichi-gatsu じゅういちがつ
12	jūni-ji じゅうにじ	15	jūgo-fun じゅうごふん	12	jūni-gatsu じゅうにがつ
?	nan-ji なんじ	20	nijup-pun にじゅっぷん	?	nan-gatsu なんがつ
		25	nijūgo-fun にじゅうごふん		
		30	sanjup-pun, han さんじゅっぷん, はん		
		?	nan-pun なんぶん		

hizuke ひづけ *date*

month		hi ひ *day*			
January	1	tsuitachi ついたち *the first day of a month*	17	jūshichi-nichi じゅうしちにち	
February	2	futsu-ka ふつか	18	jūhachi-nichi じゅうはちにち	
March	3	mik-ka みっか	19	jūku-nichi じゅうくにち	
April	4	yok-ka よっか	20	hatsu-ka はつか	
May	5	itsu-ka いつか	21	nijūichi-nichi にじゅういちにち	
June	6	mui-ka むいか	22	nijūni-nichi にじゅうににち	
July	7	nano-ka なのか	23	nijūsan-nichi にじゅうさんにち	
August	8	yō-ka ようか	24	nijūyok-ka にじゅうよっか	
September	9	kokono-ka ここのか	25	nijūgo-nichi にじゅうごにち	
October	10	tō-ka とおか	26	nijūroku-nichi にじゅうろくにち	
November	11	jūichi-nichi じゅういちにち	27	nijūshichi-nichi にじゅうしちにち	
December	12	jūni-nichi じゅうににち	28	nijūhachi-nichi にじゅうはちにち	
which month	13	jūsan-nichi じゅうさんにち	29	nijūku-nichi にじゅうくにち	
	14	jūyok-ka じゅうよっか	30	sanjū-nichi さんじゅうにち	
	15	jūgo-nichi じゅうごにち	31	sanjūichi-nichi さんじゅういちにち	
	16	jūroku-nichi じゅうろくにち	?	nan-nichi なんにち	

jikan じかん *time duration*

	hour	*minute*	*day*
1	ichi-jikan いちじかん *one hour*	ip-pun いっぷん *one minute*	ichi-nichi いちにち *one day*
2	ni-jikan にじかん	ni-fun にふん	futsu-ka ふつか
3	san-jikan さんじかん	san-pun さんぷん	mik-ka みっか
4	yo-jikan よじかん	yon-pun よんぷん	yok-ka よっか
5	go-jikan ごじかん	go-fun ごふん	itsu-ka いつか
6	roku-jikan ろくじかん	rop-pun ろっぷん	mui-ka むいか
7	nana-jikan ななじかん shichi-jikan しちじかん	nana-fun ななふん	nano-ka なのか
8	hachi-jikan はちじかん	hap-pun はっぷん hachi-fun はちふん	yō-ka ようか
9	ku-jikan くじかん	kyū-fun きゅうふん	kokono-ka ここのか
10	jū-jikan じゅうじかん	jup-pun じゅっぷん	tō-ka とおか
?	nan-jikan なんじかん	nan-pun なんぷん	nan-nichi なんにち

— 94 —

kikan きかん *period*

week	*month*	*year*
is-shūkan いっしゅうかん *one week*	ik-kagetsu いっかげつ *one month*	ichi-nen いちねん *one year*
ni-shūkan にしゅうかん	ni-kagetsu にかげつ	ni-nen にねん
san-shūkan さんしゅうかん	san-kagetsu さんかげつ	san-nen さんねん
yon-shūkan よんしゅうかん	yon-kagetsu よんかげつ	yo-nen よねん
go-shūkan ごしゅうかん	go-kagetsu ごかげつ	go-nen ごねん
roku-shūkan ろくしゅうかん	rok-kagetsu ろっかげつ han-toshi はんとし	roku-nen ろくねん
nana-shūkan ななしゅうかん	nana-kagetsu ななかげつ shichi-kagetsu しちかげつ	nana-nen ななねん shichi-nen しちねん
has-shūkan はっしゅうかん	hak-kagetsu はっかげつ	hachi-nen はちねん
kyū-shūkan きゅうしゅうかん	kyū-kagetsu きゅうかげつ	kyū-nen きゅうねん ku-nen くねん
jus-shūkan じゅっしゅうかん	juk-kagetsu じゅっかげつ	jū-nen じゅうねん
nan-shūkan なんしゅうかん	nan-kagetsu なんかげつ	nan-nen なんねん

	thing		small thing e.g. egg, orange		person	
1	hitotsu	ひとつ	ik-ko	いっこ	hitori	ひとり
2	futatsu	ふたつ	ni-ko	にこ	futari	ふたり
3	mittsu	みっつ	san-ko	さんこ	san-nin	さんにん
4	yottsu	よっつ	yon-ko	よんこ	yo-nin	よにん
5	itsutsu	いつつ	go-ko	ごこ	go-nin	ごにん
6	muttsu	むっつ	rok-ko	ろっこ	roku-nin	ろくにん
7	nanatsu	ななつ	nana-ko	ななこ	nana-nin shichi-nin	ななにん しちにん
8	yattsu	やっつ	hak-ko	はっこ	hachi-nin	はちにん
9	kokonotsu	ここのつ	kyū-ko	きゅうこ	kyū-nin ku-nin	きゅうにん くにん
10	tō	とお	juk-ko	じゅっこ	jū-nin	じゅうにん
?	ikutsu	いくつ	nan-ko	なんこ	nan-nin	なんにん

	long thing e.g. pencil, bottle		thin thing e.g. paper, plate		book	
1	ip-pon	いっぽん	ichi-mai	いちまい	is-satsu	いっさつ
2	ni-hon	にほん	ni-mai	にまい	ni-satsu	にさつ
3	san-bon	さんぼん	san-mai	さんまい	san-satsu	さんさつ
4	yon-hon	よんほん	yon-mai	よんまい	yon-satsu	よんさつ
5	go-hon	ごほん	go-mai	ごまい	go-satsu	ごさつ
6	rop-pon	ろっぽん	roku-mai	ろくまい	roku-satsu	ろくさつ
7	nana-hon	ななほん	nana-mai	ななまい	nana-satsu	ななさつ
8	hap-pon	はっぽん	hachi-mai	はちまい	has-satsu	はっさつ
9	kyū-hon	きゅうほん	kyū-mai	きゅうまい	kyū-satsu	きゅうさつ
10	jup-pon	じゅっぽん	jū-mai	じゅうまい	jus-satsu	じゅっさつ
?	nan-bon	なんぼん	nan-mai	なんまい	nan-satsu	なんさつ

auxiliary numerals 1

age		small animal etc. e.g. cat, fish		big animal etc. e.g. cow, elephant	
is-sai	いっさい	ip-piki	いっぴき	it-tō	いっとう
ni-sai	にさい	ni-hiki	にひき	ni-tō	にとう
san-sai	さんさい	san-biki	さんびき	san-tō	さんとう
yon-sai	よんさい	yon-hiki	よんひき	yon-tō	よんとう
go-sai	ごさい	go-hiki	ごひき	go-tō	ごとう
roku-sai	ろくさい	rop-piki	ろっぴき	roku-tō	ろくとう
nana-sai	ななさい	nana-hiki	ななひき	nana-tō	ななとう
has-sai	はっさい	hap-piki	はっぴき	hat-tō	はっとう
kyū-sai	きゅうさい	kyū-hiki	きゅうひき	kyū-tō	きゅうとう
jus-sai	じゅっさい	jup-piki	じゅっぴき	jut-tō	じゅっとう
nan-sai [o-]ikutsu	なんさい [お]いくつ	nan-biki	なんびき	nan-tō	なんとう

shoes, socks, etc.		drinks and so on which are in cups etc.		vehicle, machinery	
is-soku	いっそく	ip-pai	いっぱい	ichi-dai	いちだい
ni-soku	にそく	ni-hai	にはい	ni-dai	にだい
san-zoku	さんぞく	san-bai	さんばい	san-dai	さんだい
yon-soku	よんそく	yon-hai	よんはい	yon-dai	よんだい
go-soku	ごそく	go-hai	ごはい	go-dai	ごだい
roku-soku	ろくそく	rop-pai	ろっぱい	roku-dai	ろくだい
nana-soku	ななそく	nana-hai	ななはい	nana-dai	ななだい
has-soku	はっそく	hap-pai	はっぱい	hachi-dai	はちだい
kyū-soku	きゅうそく	kyū-hai	きゅうはい	kyū-dai	きゅうだい
jus-soku	じゅっそく	jup-pai	じゅっぱい	jū-dai	じゅうだい
nan-zoku	なんぞく	nan-bai	なんばい	nan-dai	なんだい

josūshi じょすうし *auxiliary numerals 2*

	ship		house		money	
1	is-seki	いっせき	ik-ken	いっけん	ichi-en	いちえん
2	ni-seki	にせき	ni-ken	にけん	ni-en	にえん
3	san-seki	さんせき	san-gen	さんげん	san-en	さんえん
4	yon-seki	よんせき	yon-ken	よんけん	yo-en	よえん
5	go-seki	ごせき	go-ken	ごけん	go-en	ごえん
6	roku-seki	ろくせき	rok-ken	ろっけん	roku-en	ろくえん
7	nana-seki	ななせき	nana-ken	ななけん	nana-en	ななえん
8	has-seki	はっせき	hak-ken	はっけん	hachi-en	はちえん
9	kyū-seki	きゅうせき	kyū-ken	きゅうけん	kyū-en	きゅうえん
10	jus-seki	じゅっせき	juk-ken	じゅっけん	jū-en	じゅうえん
?	nan-seki	なんせき	nan-gen	なんげん	ikura	いくら

	frequency		order		floor of a building	
1	ik-kai (ichi-do	いっかい いちど)	ichi-ban	いちばん	ik-kai	いっかい
2	ni-kai	にかい	ni-ban	にばん	ni-kai	にかい
3	san-kai	さんかい	san-ban	さんばん	san-gai	さんがい
4	yon-kai	よんかい	yon-ban	よんばん	yon-kai	よんかい
5	go-kai	ごかい	go-ban	ごばん	go-kai	ごかい
6	rok-kai	ろっかい	roku-ban	ろくばん	rok-kai	ろっかい
7	nana-kai	ななかい	nana-ban	ななばん	nana-kai	ななかい
8	hak-kai	はっかい	hachi-ban	はちばん	hak-kai	はっかい
9	kyū-kai	きゅうかい	kyū-ban	きゅうばん	kyū-kai	きゅうかい
10	juk-kai	じゅっかい	jū-ban	じゅうばん	juk-kai	じゅっかい
?	nan-kai (nan-do	なんかい なんど)	nan-ban	なんばん	nan-gai	なんがい

kazoku かぞく *family*

humble *e.g.* watashi no 〜 わたしの 〜 my 〜		*honorific* *e.g.* anata no 〜 あなたの 〜 your 〜		*meaning*
chichi	ちち	otōsan	おとうさん	*father*
haha	はは	okāsan	おかあさん	*mother*
ryōshin	りょうしん	go-ryōshin	ごりょうしん	*parents*
shujin otto	しゅじん} おっと	go-shujin	ごしゅじん	*husband*
kanai tsuma	かない} つま	okusan	おくさん	*wife*
ani	あに	oniisan	おにいさん	*elder brother*
ane	あね	onēsan	おねえさん	*elder sister*
otōto	おとうと	otōtosan	おとうとさん	*younger brother*
imōto	いもうと	imōtosan	いもうとさん	*younger sister*
kyōdai	きょうだい	go-kyōdai	ごきょうだい	*brother and sister*
musuko	むすこ	musukosan	むすこさん	*son*
musume	むすめ	musumesan	むすめさん	*daughter*
sofu	そふ	ojiisan	おじいさん	*grandfather*
sobo	そぼ	obāsan	おばあさん	*grandmother*
oji	おじ	ojisan	おじさん	*uncle*
oba	おば	obasan	おばさん	*aunt*
oi	おい	oigosan	おいごさん	*nephew*
mei	めい	meigosan	めいごさん	*niece*
itoko	いとこ	itoko no kata	いとこの かた	*cousin*
shinseki shinrui	しんせき} しんるい	go-shinseki go-shinrui	ごしんせき} ごしんるい	*relative*
kazoku	かぞく	go-kazoku	ごかぞく	*family*

APPENDIX 2

Conjugated Forms of Verbs

Dai I Gurūpu

masu-kei ますけい	jisho-kei じしょけい	nai-kei ないけい	te-kei てけい
aimasu あいます	au	awanai	atte
araimasu あらいます	arau	arawanai	aratte
arimasu あります	aru	nai	atte
arukimasu あるきます	aruku	arukanai	aruite
asobimasu あそびます	asobu	asobanai	asonde
chigaimasu ちがいます	chigau	chigawanai	chigatte
dashimasu だします	dasu	dasanai	dashite
furimasu [ame ga —] ふります [あめが —]	furu	furanai	futte
ganbarimasu がんばります	ganbaru	ganbaranai	ganbatte
hairimasu はいります	hairu	hairanai	haitte
hanashimasu はなします	hanasu	hanasanai	hanashite
haraimasu はらいます	harau	harawanai	haratte
hatarakimasu はたらきます	hataraku	hatarakanai	hataraite
hikimasu ひきます	hiku	hikanai	hiite
iimasu いいます	iu	iwanai	itte
ikimasu いきます	iku	ikanai	itte
irasshaimasu いらっしゃいます	irassharu	irassharanai	irasshatte
irimasu いります	iru	iranai	itte
isogimasu いそぎます	isogu	isoganai	isoide

katei-kei......conditional form
ikō-kei ......volitional form
(plain-form of -mashō)

katei-kei かていけい	ikō-kei いこうけい	imi いみ	ka か
aeba	aō	meet	8
araeba	araō	wash	18
areba	arō	have, there is	9, 10
arukeba	arukō	walk	16
asobeba	asobō	play, enjoy oneself	13
chigaeba	chigaō	differ from, be wrong	3
daseba	dasō	send (a letter), take out	13, 17
fureba	furō	rain	14
ganbareba	ganbarō	do one's best	24
haireba	hairō	enter	13
hanaseba	hanasō	speak	14
haraeba	haraō	pay	16
hatarakeba	hatarakō	work	4
hikeba	hikō	catch cold. play (the guiter), pull	9, 18, 25
ieba	iō	say, tell	14
ikeba	ikō	go	5
irasshareba	irassharō	go, come, be (honorific)	18, 27
ireba	irō	need, be necessary	16
isogeba	isogō	hurry	14

masu-kei ますけい	jisho-kei じしょけい	nai-kei ないけい	te-kei てけい
kaerimasu かえります	kaeru	kaeranai	kaette
kaeshimasu かえします	kaesu	kaesanai	kaeshite
kaimasu かいます	kau	kawanai	katte
kakarimasu かかります	kakaru	kakaranai	kakatte
kakimasu かきます	kaku	kakanai	kaite
kashimasu かします	kasu	kasanai	kashite
kawakimasu [nodo ga —] かわきます [のどが —]	kawaku	kawakanai	kawaite
keshimasu けします	kesu	kesanai	keshite
kikimasu ききます	kiku	kikanai	kiite
kirimasu きります	kiru	kiranai	kitte
komarimasu こまります	komaru	komaranai	komatte
kudasaimasu くださいます	kudasaru	kudasaranai	kudasatte
machimasu まちます	matsu	matanai	matte
magarimasu まがります	magaru	magaranai	magatte
meshiagarimasu めしあがります	meshiagaru	meshiagaranai	meshiagatte
mochimasu もちます	motsu	motanai	motte
moraimasu もらいます	morau	morawanai	moratte
motte ikimasu もって いきます	motte iku	motte ikanai	motte itte
nakushimasu なくします	nakusu	nakusanai	nakushite
naorimasu なおります	naoru	naoranai	naotte
naoshimasu なおします	naosu	naosanai	naoshite
naraimasu ならいます	narau	narawanai	naratte
narimasu なります	naru	naranai	natte
nomimasu のみます	nomu	nomanai	nonde

katei-kei かていけい	ikō-kei いこうけい	imi いみ	ka か
kaereba	kaerō	go home	5
kaeseba	kaesō	return (give back)	16
kaeba	kaō	buy	6
kakareba	kakarō	it takes ... (time)	6
kakeba	kakō	write, paint	6, 24
kaseba	kasō	lend	7
kawakeba	kawakō	be thirsty	13
keseba	kesō	put out, switch off, erase	15
kikeba	kikō	listen, ask	6, 19
kireba	kirō	cut	7
komareba	komarō	be troubled	16
kudasareba	kudasarō	give me (honorific)	27
mateba	matō	wait	14
magareba	magarō	turn, bend	22
meshiagareba	meshiagarō	eat, drink (honorific)	27
moteba	motō	hold	15
moraeba	moraō	receive, be given	7
motte ikeba	motte ikō	take something with someone	17
nakuseba	nakusō	lose	17
naoreba	naorō	get well, be repaired	17
naoseba	naosō	repair, correct, cure	18
naraeba	naraō	learn	7
nareba	narō	become	15
nomeba	nomō	drink	6

masu-kei ますけい	jisho-kei じしょけい	nai-kei ないけい	te-kei てけい
norimasu のります	noru	noranai	notte
nugimasu ぬぎます	nugu	nuganai	nuide
okimasu おきます	oku	okanai	oite
okurimasu おくります	okuru	okuranai	okutte
omoimasu おもいます	omou	omowanai	omotte
oshimasu おします	osu	osanai	oshite
osshaimasu おっしゃいます	ossharu	ossharanai	osshatte
owarimasu おわります	owaru	owaranai	owatte
oyogimasu およぎます	oyogu	oyoganai	oyoide
sawarimasu さわります	sawaru	sawaranai	sawatte
shirimasu しります	shiru	shiranai	shitte
suimasu [tabako o —] すいます [タバコを —]	suu	su·wanai	sutte
sukimasu [onaka ga —] すきます [おなかが —]	suku	sukanai	suite
sumimasu すみます	sumu	sumanai	sunde
suwarimasu すわります	suwaru	suwaranai	suwatte
tachimasu たちます	tatsu	tatanai	tatte
tetsudaimasu てつだいます	tetsudau	tetsudawanai	tetsudatte
tomarimasu とまります	tomaru	tomaranai	tomatte
torimasu とります	toru	toranai	totte
tsukaimasu つかいます	tsukau	tsukawanai	tsukatte
tsukimasu つきます	tsuku	tsukanai	tsuite
tsukurimasu つくります	tsukuru	tsukuranai	tsukutte
ugokimasu うごきます	ugoku	ugokanai	ugoite
urimasu うります	uru	uranai	utte

katei-kei かていけい	ikō-kei いこうけい	imi いみ	ka か
noreba	norō	ride, get on	16
nugeba	nugō	take off	17
okeba	okō	put	15
okureba	okurō	send	7
omoeba	omoō	think	21
oseba	osō	push, press	25
osshareba	ossharō	say (honorific)	27
owareba	owarō	come or bring to an end	6
oyogeba	oyogō	swim	18
sawareba	sawarō	touch	17
shireba	shirō	get to know, find out	15
sueba	suō	smoke	6
sukeba	sukō	be hungry	13
sumeba	sumō	live	15
suwareba	suwarō	sit down	15
tateba	tatō	stand up	14
tetsudaeba	tetsudaō	help (to do), assist	15
tomareba	tomarō	stop (v.i.), stay (at hotel)	16, 19
toreba	torō	take	6, 14
tsukaeba	tsukaō	use	15
tsukeba	tsukō	arrive, be turned on	7, 25
tsukureba	tsukurō	make, produce	11
ugokeba	ugokō	move	25
ureba	urō	sell	15

masu-kei ますけい	jisho-kei じしょけい	nai-kei ないけい	te-kei てけい
utaimasu うたいます	utau	utawanai	utatte
wakarimasu わかります	wakaru	wakaranai	wakatte
waraimasu わらいます	warau	warawanai	waratte
watarimasu わたります	wataru	wataranai	watatte
yaku ni tachimasu やくに たちます	yaku ni tatsu	yaku ni tatanai	yaku ni tatte
yasumimasu やすみます	yasumu	yasumanai	yasunde
yobimasu よびます	yobu	yobanai	yonde
yomimasu よみます	yomu	yomanai	yonde

Dai II Gurūpu

masu-kei ますけい	jisho-kei じしょけい	nai-kei ないけい	te-kei てけい
abimasu [shawā o —] あびます [シャワーを —]	abiru	abinai	abite
agemasu あげます	ageru	agenai	agete
akemasu あけます	akeru	akenai	akete
dekakemasu でかけます	dekakeru	dekakenai	dekakete
dekimasu できます	dekiru	dekinai	dekite
demasu でます	deru	denai	dete
hajimemasu はじめます	hajimeru	hajimenai	hajimete
imasu います	iru	inai	ite
iremasu いれます	ireru	irenai	irete
kaemasu かえます	kaeru	kaenai	kaete
kakemasu [denwa o —] かけます [でんわを —]	kakeru	kakenai	kakete
kangaemasu かんがえます	kangaeru	kangaenai	kangaete
karimasu かります	kariru	karinai	karite

katei-kei かていけい	ikō-kei いこうけい	imi いみ	ka か
utaeba	utaō	sing	18
wakareba	wakarō	understand	9
waraeba	waraō	laugh, smile	17
watareba	watarō	cross	22
yaku ni tateba	yaku ni tatō	be useful	16
yasumeba	yasumō	rest, be absent	4, 9
yobeba	yobō	call, invite	14
yomeba	yomō	read	6

katei-kei かていけい	ikō-kei いこうけい	imi いみ	ka か
abireba	abiyō	take shower	18
agereba	ageyō	give	7
akereba	akeyō	open	15
dekakereba	dekakeyō	go out (of house)	18
dekireba	dekiyō	can, be formed	18, 26
dereba	deyō	go out	13
hajimereba	hajimeyō	begin	6
ireba	iyō	there is, be, stay	10, 11
irereba	ireyō	put in	17
kaereba	kaeyō	change	13
kakereba	kakeyō	phone	7
kangaereba	kangaeyō	consider, think	25
karireba	kariyō	borrow	18

masu-kei ますけい	jisho-kei じしょけい	nai-kei ないけい	te-kei てけい
kiemasu きえます	kieru	kienai	kiete
kikoemasu きこえます	kikoeru	kikoenai	kikoete
kimasu きます	kiru	kinai	kite
ki o tsukemasu きを つけます	ki o tsukeru	ki o tsukenai	ki o tsukete
kumitatemasu くみたてます	kumitateru	kumitatenai	kumitatete
miemasu みえます	mieru	mienai	miete
mimasu みます	miru	minai	mite
misemasu みせます	miseru	misenai	misete
nemasu ねます	neru	nenai	nete
norikaemasu のりかえます	norikaeru	norikaenai	norikaete
oboemasu おぼえます	oboeru	oboenai	oboete
okimasu おきます	okiru	okinai	okite
orimasu おります	oriru	orinai	orite
oshiemasu おしえます	oshieru	oshienai	oshiete
shimemasu しめます	shimeru	shimenai	shimete
shirabemasu しらべます	shiraberu	shirabenai	shirabete
tabemasu たべます	taberu	tabenai	tabete
tomemasu とめます	tomeru	tomenai	tomete
tsukaremasu つかれます	tsukareru	tsukarenai	tsukarete
tsukemasu つけます	tsukeru	tsukenai	tsukete
umaremasu うまれます	umareru	umarenai	umarete
wasuremasu わすれます	wasureru	wasurenai	wasurete
yamemasu やめます	yameru	yamenai	yamete

katei-kei かていけい	ikō-kei いこうけい	imi いみ	ka か
kiereba	kieyō	go out, put out	25
kikoereba	kikoeyō	be audible, (can) be heard	26
kireba	kiyō	wear	15
ki o tsukereba	ki o tsukeyō	pay attention	17
kumitatereba	kumitateyō	assemble	24
miereba	mieyō	be visible, (can) be seen	26
mireba	miyō	look (at), see	6
misereba	miseyō	show	14
nereba	neyō	sleep	4
norikaereba	norikaeyō	change (trains)	22
oboereba	oboeyō	memorize	14
okireba	okiyō	get up	4
orireba	oriyō	get off	16
oshiereba	oshieyō	teach, tell	7, 14
shimereba	shimeyō	shut, close	15
shirabereba	shirabeyō	check, investigate	25
tabereba	tabeyō	eat	6
tomereba	tomeyō	stop (vt.)	17
tsukarereba	tsukareyō	be tired	13
tsukereba	tsukeyō	switch on	15
umarereba	umareyō	be born	23
wasurereba	wasureyō	forget	17
yamereba	yameyō	give up, stop, quit	19

Dai III Gurūpu

masu-kei ますけい	jisho-kei じしょけい	nai-kei ないけい	te-kei てけい
benkyō-shimasu べんきょうします	benkyō-suru	benkyō-shinai	benkyō-shite
bunkai-shimasu ぶんかいします	bunkai-suru	bunkai-shinai	bunkai-shite
chōsetsu-shimasu ちょうせつします	chōsetsu-suru	chōsetsu-shinai	chōsetsu-shite
chūi-shimasu ちゅういします	chūi-suru	chūi-shinai	chūi-shite
jisshū-shimasu じっしゅうします	jisshū-suru	jisshū-shinai	jisshū-shite
kaimono-shimasu かいものします	kaimono-suru	kaimono-shinai	kaimono-shite
kekkon-shimasu けっこんします	kekkon-suru	kekkon-shinai	kekkon-shite
kenbutsu-shimasu けんぶつします	kenbutsu-suru	kenbutsu-shinai	kenbutsu-shite
kengaku-shimasu けんがくします	kengaku-suru	kengaku-shinai	kengaku-shite
kimasu きます	kuru	konai	kite
koshō-shimasu こしょうします	koshō-suru	koshō-shinai	koshō-shite
motte kimasu もって きます	motte kuru	motte konai	motte kite
nokku-shimasu ノックします	nokku-suru	nokku-shinai	nokku-shite
onegai-shimasu おねがいします	onegai-suru	onegai-shinai	onegai-shite
pinpon-shimasu ピンポンします	pinpon-suru	pinpon-shinai	pinpon-shite
sanpo-shimasu さんぽします	sanpo-suru	sanpo-shinai	sanpo-shite
sentaku-shimasu せんたくします	sentaku-suru	sentaku-shinai	sentaku-shite
setsumei-shimasu せつめいします	setsumei-suru	setsumei-shinai	setsumei-shite
shimasu します	suru	shinai	shite
shinpai-shimasu しんぱいします	shinpai-suru	shinpai-shinai	shinpai-shite
shitsumon-shimasu しつもんします	shitsumon-suru	shitsumon-shinai	shitsumon-shite
shitsurei-shimasu しつれいします	shitsurei-suru	shitsurei-shinai	shitsurei-shite
shokuji-shimasu しょくじします	shokuji-suru	shokuji-shinai	shokuji-shite

katei-kei かていけい	ikō-kei いこうけい	imi いみ	ka か
benkyō-sureba	benkyō-shiyō	study	4
bunkai-sureba	bunkai-shiyō	disassemble, take to pieces	24
chōsetsu- sureba	chōsetsu-shiyō	adjust	26
chūi-sureba	chūi-shiyō	pay attention	22
jisshū-sureba	jisshū-shiyō	have a practical training	6
kaimono- sureba	kaimono-shiyō	do shopping	13
kekkon-sureba	kekkon-shiyō	marry	13
kenbutsu- sureba	kenbutsu- shiyō	do sightseeing	13
kengaku- sureba	kengaku-shiyō	observe for study, visit	13
kureba	koyō	come	5
koshō-sureba	koshō-shiyō	be out of order	18
motte kureba	motte koyō	bring	17
nokku-sureba	nokku-shiyō	knock	18
onegai-sureba	onegai-shiyō	ask, request	7
pinpon-sureba	pinpon-shiyō	play pingpong	6
sanpo-sureba	sanpo-shiyō	take a walk	13
sentaku- sureba	sentaku-shiyō	wash clothes	11
setsumei- sureba	setsumei- shiyō	explain	24
sureba	shiyō	do	6
shinpai-sureba	shinpai-shiyō	worry	17
shitsumon- sureba	shitsumon- shiyō	ask a question	23
shitsurei- sureba	shitsurei-shiyō	excuse me	19
shokuji-sureba	shokuji-shiyō	take meals, dine	26

masu-kei ますけい	jisho-kei じしょけい	nai-kei ないけい	te-kei てけい
shūrl-shimasu しゅうりします	shūri-suru	shūri-shinai	shūri-shite
sōji-shimasu そうじします	sōji-suru	sōji-shinai	sōji-shite
sōsa-shimasu そうさします	sōsa-suru	sōsa-shınai	sōsa-shite
unten-shimasu うんてんします	unten-suru	unten-shinai	unten-shite

katei-kei かていけい	ikō-kei いこうけい	imi いみ	ka か
shūri-sureba	shūri-shiyō	repair	7
sōji-sureba	sōji-shiyō	clean	11
sōsa-sureba	sōsa-shiyō	operate	26
unten-sureba	unten-shiyō	drive	18

日 本 語 の 基 礎 I
＜分冊 英語訳＞
定価1,130円(本体1,097円)

1973年8月31日　初版発行
1989年6月15日　第13刷

編　集　　財団法人 海外技術者研修協会
発　行　　株式会社 スリー エー ネットワーク
　　　　　東京都千代田区猿楽町2丁目6番3号
　　　　　電話 03(292)5751(代表)　　松栄ビル
　　　　　郵便番号　101

印　刷　　日 本 印 刷 株 式 会 社

不許複製　ISBN4-906224-03-2 C0081